The
Retirement
Money Book

Rustproof Your Retirement

Retirement
doesn't have to be
a red light.

It can be
a green light.
Othmar Ammann
would agree.

After he "retired"
at age 60,
he designed,
among other things,
the Connecticut and
New Jersey Turnpikes;
the Pittsburgh Civic Arena;
Dulles Airport;
the Throgs Neck Bridge;
and the
Verrazano Narrows Bridge.

Paul Gauguin "retired"
as a successful stockbroker
and became
a world-famous artist.

Heinrich Schliemann
"retired" from business
to look for Homer's
legendary city of
Troy.
He found it.

After Churchill made his
mark as a world statesman,
he picked up
his pen and won the
Nobel Prize for Literature
at age 79.

Don't just go fishing
when you retire.
Go hunting.
Hunt for the chance
to do what
you've always
wanted to do.
Then go do it!

Reprinted with permission of Harry J. Gray, Chairman and Chief Executive
Officer, United Technologies, Box 360, Hartford, CT 06141

The Retirement Money Book

Ferd Nauheim

ACROPOLIS BOOKS LTD.
Washington, D.C. 20009

ACROPOLIS BOOKS LTD.
Colortone Building, 2400 17th St., N.W.
Washington, D.C. 20009

Printed in the United States of America by
COLORTONE PRESS Creative Graphics, Inc.
Washington, D.C. 20009

This publication is designed to provide accurate
and authoritative information in regard to the
subject matter covered. It is sold with the
understanding that the publisher is not engaged
in rendering legal, accounting or other
professional service. If legal advice or other
professional assistance is required, the services of
a competent professional person should be
sought.

Library of Congress Cataloging in Publication Data

Nauheim, Ferd.
    The retirement money book.

    Includes index.
    1. Finance, Personal. 2. Retirement income.
I. Title.
HG179.N374   332.024'01   81-14940
ISBN 0-87491-437-X   AACR2

For Bea,
with loving gratitude
for her mental and manual contributions.

Contents

Invading capital once was a sin; today it usually is a *must* . . . In retirement judicious spending is more important than saving . . . Reinvestment programs and the payment of premiums on cash value life insurance are forms of saving . . . . Life insurance cash values should be used . . . Beware of "safe havens"; the guarantees they offer may be guaranteed losses . . . When and how to take Social Security . . . The vital need to be in control . . . No business can operate without a financial statement, and you are in the critical business of how you'll live the rest of your life . . . Simple balance sheet forms you can use.

Common stocks for "Total Return" . . . Which stocks?
. . . Choosing a broker . . . 6 rules for investing on
your own . . . Where do you look for growth? . . .
What the record of the past 15 years reveals . . . The
Pied Pipers of Panic . . . The big benefits in common
stock ownership . . . Where to seek help . . . Mutual
funds: the traditional funds, the money market funds,
the tax-free income funds . . . Withdrawal plans and
other fund services . . . Preferred stocks . . . Convertible bonds . . . Options . . . EE and HH Bonds.

Chapter Five
How a Retired Person
Should Invest

(*Special Feature*—Interview with Gail Winslow, vice-
chairman of a New York Stock Exchange firm, one of
the best known and most highly respected women
brokers in the United States.)

The need to simplify . . . Perhaps you should move to
a new advisor . . . Out of the safe-deposit box to a
broker's safe-keeping . . . Putting your stocks in
"street name" . . . Bringing your records up-to-date
. . . End speculation and find ways to conserve . . .
Gail Winslow's 5 points for investing in retirement.

Chapter Six
More Income Through
Real Estate

Capitalizing on your own home . . . The "reverse mortgage" . . . Sale/Leasebacks . . . Refinancing . . . Paying if off . . . Tax-favored rollover . . . $125,000 tax-
free gain . . . Renting your home . . . Sell and take second mortgage . . . Sell and take first mortgage . . .
Installment sale . . . Wipe out mortgage, remain in
your home, and get income tax deductions—all
through a Life Estaté Agreement . . . Using a

cumstances . . . Longevity: a retirement financing problem . . . Importance of growth along with income . . . Need for "cost of living" increases . . . Using growth investments to produce current income . . . Emotional aspects that underscore need for professional help . . . Payout from pension plans in early years, creating an untaxed source of capital as basis for planning opportunities . . . Invasion of capital gains vs invasion of capital . . . Plan that you will live beyond normal life expectancy . . . The relative importance of liquidity . . . Borrowing as an approach to liquidity.

Introduction

About
This Book —

You are absolutely right! You're reading this book because you're concerned about the economy in general and how you can add some lustre to your own financial future in particular. And you *should* be concerned about your financial future because you *can* do a great deal to improve it.

The Retirement Money Book is dedicated to the choices and opportunities you have to shape your retirement years to your own liking. As you move through the following pages, you will find countless ideas you can use right now...ways to increase your spending money... ways to increase your capital...ways to make your retirement years productive and rewarding...ways to make retirement a graduation to something better.

You're going to see reasons why you should change your thinking about money and financial products and services. You will discover fresh ways to look at "safe havens" and risks for your money. You'll learn to make personal financial plans that aim directly at solid, realizable goals. You'll find out what you can do to protect what you have while using all the resources at your disposal to rid yourself of financial worry and uncertainty. You will learn to recognize what costly types of protection are no longer needed and why.

Taxes can play an important role in what lies ahead in your financial future. You will find that there are a number of ways to side-step, reduce or postpone giving your money to the tax collector.

And don't for a moment think that you can't take aggressive action to increase your spending money. There are a variety of ways to uncover hidden assets... capital you didn't know you had or thought was out of reach. For example, you will read about a couple living in a home they loved, saddled with heavy mortgage payments and taxes and how they took measures that eliminated the mortgage, reduced their taxes and guaranteed that the home would always be theirs to live in.

Many people fear inflation more than anything else. Now you can stop fearing and start fighting.

Read, consider and choose what you can do to live your life with happiness, dignity and comfort. There is much enjoyment in store for many who believed that retirement would be a period of emptiness. It does not have to be. There are just too many ways to make those years a time of doing the things you always hoped you might without having economic uncertainties interfere.

Reading this book should be a voyage of learning and hope. If you end that journey with just a few ideas that you can use... just two or three out of the scores that will unfold... the rewards can be immense. Start reading with the conviction that you can bless your future with accomplishment and contentment. If you read with that thought in mind, you will be absolutely right.

Ferd Nauheim

Chapter One

You Have To Change Your Mind

Three things can help to make your retirement years as rewarding as you want them to be. First: enough spending money to enable you to live those years without having to reduce your living standards, without frustration and without fear. Second: a stimulating activity of your choosing. Third: good health. Physicians, psychologists, psychiatrists, geriatric specialists and people in retirement agree that if you have the first two the chances of your enjoying good health are significantly increased.

Whether you are planning for retirement or you are already there and want to give yourself some better weapons to fight the financial battle and to improve the quality of your life, you will recognize that many of the money management ideas you will be reading about are applicable. Your own special circumstances might move you to pay particular attention to a thought addressed to the people on the other side of the retirement line.

15

The big common factor, whether you are preparing to retire or have actually retired, is the need to change your thinking. We've all been raised with certain teachings, preachings, beliefs, solemn warnings, near sacred adages, powerful convictions and wholehearted prejudices about dealing with money. They are deeply ingrained. They are difficult to uproot and throw out, but the successful management of money in the retirement years, in an inflationary economy, demands that you make up your mind to change your mind.

A few examples: Do you hold to the belief that it is practically a sin to invade your capital? In retirement it can be a greater sin not to do so. You are going to see some eye-opening examples of how the knowledgeable invasion of capital can be enormously beneficial to you. Is it your practice to shun the use of credit...to think that credit is something to be avoided by retirees? You are going to be shown some very sound reasons to modify that belief. Is it your conviction that the only intelligent way to handle money is to faithfully route a part of all income to savings? You will see why it will pay you to rid yourself of that thought. Have you always felt that in retirement the pursuit of income is the only sensible investment objective? Not so. And you'll be shown why. Has it been your impression that participation in financial projects designed to avoid or reduce taxes are unpatriotic and somewhat shady? Far from the truth. You'll discover ways of dealing with taxes that are totally aboveboard and, importantly, helpful to you. Do you hold that the compounding of interest, dividends and realized capital gains are vital to the building and conservation of capital? The opposite can be true. Do you think that after retiring when you no longer have the earned income you enjoyed at your earning peak you must cut back on charitable contributions? You are going to find out that some ways of making the biggest charitable gifts of your life can increase your income materially. There is a lot of mind and attitude changing ahead.

Learning to accept the changes that apply to your personal situation is one of the greater rewards in store for you. Another important aim of this book is to point the way to making retirement a step up and not a step down — a graduation to a fuller, more stimulating, richer part of your life experience. It can be done. It should be done. The more you think about getting ready for the dollar needs of retirement, or how to improve your situation after retirement, the more it becomes evident that changing habitual thinking about money is an absolute must. So many things you once believed have become musty.

Consider Sarah Blume. At age seventy-two Sarah is depriving herself in a dozen different ways because her income fails to keep up with living costs. Her rent has gone through the ceiling; food costs have become a disaster and clothing prices hardly matter for she stopped buying anything new nearly three years ago. Even lunch and a movie with a friend have become so costly that she rarely indulges. But Sarah owns some stock of the company her late husband worked for. The current worth of her stock is $100,000. It pays a miserable dividend — less than 2 percent — giving her about $1,850 a year. She has some Social Security income, too. Put it all together and Sarah, who was accustomed to the good life when George was on the scene, is living on crumbs... deprived, depressed, deluded.

At the heart of her problem is that shortly before he died George said, "Sarah, never, never, never sell that stock. The company is old, solid, strong and progressive. It will keep on growing and its stock will constantly increase in value. That stock will take care of you as long as you live."

No one is going to convince Sarah that she should

sell her stock and put that money where it can earn some decent income for her. But she can and should be shown that she can have her cake and eat it too...a la mode. She can and must change her mind. George was absolutely right when he told her that the stock would grow in value over the years. It can help take care of her for as long as she lives. But he failed to tell her how to enjoy those benefits. When he said his last farewell to Sarah, the stock he left her had a market value of $47,000.

Forgive me while I have a chat with Sarah

"Sarah, you now have $100,000 worth of the stock your husband left to you. You have many more shares than he left. Some came as stock dividends and some as stock splits. Sarah, the life expectancy tables say that a female between 70 and 75 has almost 15 more years to look forward to. That is an average. Let's say that you will live another 20 years. $100,000 divided by 20 years amounts to $5,000 a year. Tell some stockbroker to sell one twentieth of your stock each year. Do that and the probability is that you can live the rest of your life in relaxed comfort. Selling one-twentieth of your stock will give you an extra $5,000 to spend this year, and in all probability, you may have still more in future years. George was right. You have stock in a fine, strong company. If inflation continues at anything like present levels there is good reason to expect that the value of your stock will match or even go ahead of increases in living costs. But if you don't really need the increases, as and if they come, you'll be wise to reduce the amount of stock you sell each year. In that way you can be certain that no matter how many years of good living you may enjoy ahead you won't outlive your money for living. Sarah, George established a source of money for you so that you can live with comfort and pleasure and be free of worry. Use it."

Inflation, the constant uncompaniable companion

There was a time when spending capital was considered reckless and foolish because capital is what produces income. That thinking changed dramatically when income, after taxes, rarely kept up with living costs. For nearly thirty years we have had inflation as a constant uncompanionable companion. The last time the cost of living went down was in 1954 when it dipped one half of one percent. You know what has happened since then. Inflation has been getting bigger and rougher until it has become regarded as the nation's number one cause for concern. Thanks to the combined pressures of inflation and high estate and income taxes it has become quite common, even for people with relatively modest assets, to use simple trusts to protect their heirs. The most common of these is the type of trust that leaves the assets to children but gives the surviving wife or husband the income from those assets for as long as that individual lives. It is an effective means of sharply reducing estate taxes because the assets are subject to those taxes only once. Without the trust, a husband leaves everything to his wife and the "everything" is taxed. Then, when she passes on, everything goes to the children and there's that tax collector holding his hand out again.

The crime of invading capital has been repealed

For a quarter of a century, or better, the most conservative of lawyers have been advising clients to add to trusts of that type, instructions that the surviving mate be given the "power of invasion." That is legal talk meaning that should the executor of the will see that the widow or widower is having a rough time getting along on the income, it is permissable to make some of the capital available. How much capital, and under what circumstances, will differ from case to case. The point is that the professionals, who usually are the ultra conservatives, have discarded the concept that it is a sin to tap one's capital. The crime of invading capital has been repealed.

For the years of high inflation
look to "total return"

Lawyers aren't the only ones with a language of their own. People in the securities business also use some strange expressions. One term they have used increasingly in these double-digit inflation years is *total return*. This is another reflection of the departure from putting a DO NOT TOUCH sign on capital. With even extraordinarily high income being incapable of matching inflation rates after income taxes are subtracted, the thinking is that one must also look for opportunities to have investments capable of growing in value. The growth in value plus the dividends or interest add up to *total return*. For example, you buy shares of PDQ stock at $20 a share. The stock pays an annual dividend of 7 percent. At the end of a year PDQ stock is $24 a share. The value has increased by 20 percent. That increase in value added to the dividend income amounts to 27 percent. That is your *total return*. How to employ *total return* is each person's own decision. It should be based on realistic needs. Sarah Blume, brutally pinched by inadequate income, was shown that she could use a generous estimate of her life expectancy to capture a combination of capital growth and dividend income. Her approach was not pegged to actual increases in capital growth and income from dividends, but on a conservative estimate of how long she might live. You can elect to use the *total return* idea by selling enough shares each year to match annual increases in value, if any. Taking more would, of course, subtract from the base producing the dividends, reducing future *total return*. Dividend income can increase or decrease. You have to consider both parts of the investment, value and dividend income, in deciding how *total return* can best serve your needs. The point is that the adoption of a *total return* strategy is still another way of turning your back on the obsolete idea that any use of capital is a no-no.

The future has arrived

Saving... another word that is revered and accepted as a sign of good American discipline, prudence and wisdom. The question is, *what are you saving for?* If you have retired, the proverbial rainy day is here. If you are doing just fine and wish to save so that you can increase what you will leave to your children, that makes sense. But if you are having problems with living costs and with the full enjoyment of life, this is not the time to save. It is the time to shift from being a saver to becoming a spender; not spending in an undisciplined manner but using what is available to you to lighten financial burdens... to give your life some mental and material relaxation. That is not an easy thing to do if you have devoted the better part of your life to disciplining yourself to save. Spending the money you customarily would have saved gives you the feeling that you are adrift. You've cut the anchor cord and are letting the currents of day-to-day life carry you as they will. The opposite is the reality.

Inflation can play havoc with what you are sending ahead

Unless you have more income than you need, a fundamental part of your financial planning must be a businesslike means of supplying yourself with all the income you can muster. If the savings habit is not broken, you are depriving yourself of current spending money and using it to provide future spending money. You are ignoring the fact that inflation can play havoc with the worth of what you are sending ahead.

After World War I, when Germany was going through one of the most terrible periods of inflation in history, working people insisted on being paid twice each day. The moment they had cash in their hands they would rush out and spend because they knew that their money would buy far less within a matter of hours. Fortunately, we aren't living in that kind of nightmare. But inflation does relentlessly reduce the value... the buying power... of our dollars. That is an important reason why most people living on unearned income, the income produced by their savings and investments, can be making a serious mistake if they deprive themselves today with the belief that the money they put into savings will produce the income that will make their lives brighter and easier in the years ahead.

Control permits changes for the better

In most cases you are better off to use available income for today's needs and comforts, always working to make your controllable sources of capital increasingly productive. While you have no control over your Social Security benefits, and some other income producers, there are income sources that you can control. Control permits changes for the better. The purpose of this book is to explore the changes you may make to enlarge your spending power and to enrich your life.

Savings take many forms. The automatic reinvestment of dividends, interest and realized profits is one way of saving. You by-pass taking those dividend, interest and realized profit distributions in cash and plow them back into whatever created them. This is compounding, and compounding is a highly desirable force during the years of accumulation. If you are financially shaky in retirement, reinvestment is undesirable. Reinvestment not only puts limits on the things you need and want today, it is almost certain to be a guaranteed way of adding to the taxes that must be paid on your estate after you are gone.

Your life insurance premiums
may include savings

Ordinary, cash value or whole life insurance, three names for the same thing, is sold on the strength of the fact that it includes automatic savings. If you have retired and continue to pay premiums on a policy of that kind, this is the time to stop. Ordinary life takes part of each premium and credits it to a *cash value* that keeps growing as long as the policy is in force and you keep sending your checks to the company.

You have two ways of using your cash value: (1) Tell the company to use your cash values to pay for a paid-up policy. The value of the policy will be reduced to some extent, depending on the amount of cash value you have accumulated. You are through paying premiums forever but the protection remains in force until you die. (2) You can instruct the company to use your cash values to buy an *extended term policy*. In this case you no longer pay any premiums but you continue to have life insurance for the same amount of protection as before. It will remain in force for a period of time based on the amount of your cash values. If you do not have enough to last to the end of the line you will run out of protection at some point. On the other hand you may have more than enough. If that is so the company will rebate to your estate any unearned premium dollars.

You have two other possibilities, and which of the two you may elect depends on the outcome of a realistic look at your need for life insurance.

Do you really need any life insurance?

During the earning years life insurance can be immensely important if there are any dependents to protect. Should the bread winner die, so does earned income. The family is caught unexpectedly. A serious income vacuum develops. Life insurance is the soundest means of protection against that financial dilemma.

In retirement the circumstances are different. In the average situation the death of a retired person does not materially reduce income. It may not reduce it at all. A further factor is that retired people seldom have any minors who depend on them for support.

Examine your own situation. Ask yourself if you really need life insurance. Some feel that it is important to have some life insurance to provide the capital that may be needed to handle final expenses and estate taxes. Maybe so, but there are a number of ways of having liquid assets that may be available for such purposes. Life insurance costs money. The alternate sources of cash to handle final expenses and taxes could be working to produce income — to increase in value.

If you decide that you do not have a genuine need for life insurance, simply cancel the policy and collect the accumulated cash value. If you conclude that there is good reason to hold on to your life insurance protection, you have one final and very interesting choice.

Borrow your cash values. This can be the most interesting option your ordinary life policy provides. It is an option that has been used by many people in recent years. The older your policy, the bigger the benefit. All ordinary life insurance contracts include an agreement that you have the right to borrow any portion or all of the cash values whenever you want. Policies that have been in effect for a fair number of years guarantee that the interest rate the company may charge will be 5 or 6 percent. More recent policies have increased that to 8 percent.

A loan that need not be repaid

The interesting thing about your borrowing the cash values in your policy is that it is unlike any other type of loan. There is no due date for repayment. The insurance company will never harrass you to pay any principal or interest. If you never repay any part of the loan or the interest, the total of the two will be deducted from the amount paid to your estate. And that should not matter. The great likelihood is that you will move the borrowed money from one place to another. To illustrate the advantages involved let's take a typical case. Bill Brown has had a $150,000 ordinary life policy for many years. The cash value has been accumulating all of that time and currently amounts to $80,000. Bill borrows the entire $80,000 and puts it where it will earn 12 percent a year for him. Between now and the time he dies he is collecting 12 percent and the insurance company is charging him 5 percent. He pays back no part of the borrowed money, nor does he pay any of the interest. When he passes on the company pays his estate $150,000 less the $80,000 and accumulated interest. But the estate also will receive the $80,000 Bill invested, and the 7 percent difference between the interest charges and the 12 percent Bill and his wife were collecting over the years more than compensates for the interest deduction.

Compare Bill's ability to borrow $80,000 at 5 percent with what he would have been required to pay had he borrowed that money from a bank.

Further along you will read about the advantages of establishing an insurance trust or of a husband giving the ownership of his insurance policies to his wife. Making use of those techniques does not eliminate the opportunity to borrow cash values. Whoever is the registered owner of a policy may borrow the money — the trust or the wife may do so.

No red tape is involved. To borrow cash values, you write to the company or call your agent, properly identify yourself and the policy, and the check will be on its way to you without delay.

Putting your money where it is safe

One attitude that is particularly difficult to change your mind about concerns the traditional *safe places* to put your money. Banks... what is safer than a bank? The Federal Deposit Insurance Corporation (FDIC), an agency of the United States Government, insures your deposits up to $100,000 and there are ways of covering larger sums with that FDIC insurance by simply having separate accounts in different names or in different banks. Wonderfully safe. Just walking into a bank and seeing all that marble, the guards and the vaults inspires you with a sense of total safety. The thrift institutions, with your deposits insured up to $100,000 by another government agency, the Federal Savings and Loan Insurance Corporation (FSLIC), also wears a great image of safety. Until recently banks and savings and loans paid no interest on checking accounts (savings and loans had no checking accounts) and very modest interest on passbook savings. When NOW (Negotiable Orders of Withdrawal) accounts became generally available in 1981, paying about 5½ percent interest, the squeeze on your checking account dollars was relieved to some extent. Certificates of Deposit and Money Market Certificates, offered to those who could adjust to the time and minimum deposit requirements, have been responsive to today's economy. But NOW account interest and passbook interest lag far behind. If your top federal income tax bracket is approximately 30 percent, your net return is less than 4 percent. For as long as inflation exceeds 4 percent you have *an unmistakable loss*. With inflation as high as 10 percent and higher, it is a serious loss. If your capital is where it is losing money, it is not realistic to call it a *safe place*. Putting money in places traditionally called *safe* can be quite reckless.

During the years when you were saving, investing and accumulating money for what future income it would produce, compounding power was powerful, helpful. Interest or dividends, kept at work, earning still more interest or dividends accelerates growth dramatically. That is well known. What is not nearly as well known is that inflation compounds in precisely the same manner and there is one staggering difference. You can call a halt to the compounding of an investment but you can do nothing about the compounding of inflation. To illustrate: suppose you bought something for $100 and for the following ten years inflation was a uniform 12 percent. You might assume that the inflated price at the end of that period would increase by ten times the inflation rate of 12 percent (10 × $12 = $120, plus the original price of $100 = $220) making the present price $220. But because inflation does compound the *new price tag would be $314.56.*

Brutal double digit inflation is not a new experience in the United States. In 1946 our inflation rate was 18.2 percent. Just after World War I it was 25 percent. Effort by the government to control inflation is not a modern historical situation either. In 301 A.D. Roman Emperor Diocletian instituted wage and price controls in his battle against run-away inflation. The penalty for violations was death. *And it still didn't work.*

While in the process of planning this book, I was working with a financial organization in Santiago, Chile for a brief period. The people of Chile were immensely pleased because their inflation had been reduced from 1,000 percent a year down to 30 percent.

I asked a young business man, "How in the world did you people manage with 1,000 percent annual inflation?"

He said, "Ferd, you must remember that we have lived with immensely high inflation for more than 40 years. You learn how to manage."

I persisted, "How did you manage?"

He replied with a single word, "Barter."

Barter, of course, is always an option, and on page 61 you'll see that there are people here in the United States who are employing barter as their personal answer to the problem. The point is that inflation and its bruising impact cannot be ignored. It must be fought and even if you do not find a way to raise your income sufficiently to equal the speed of rising living costs, at least you can blunt the blow.

What are the sources of your income?

The Social Security Bureau made a study to determine where the income of people age 65 and over came from. This is what they reported:

29% — earned income, people still working full or part time

34% — Social Security

7% — public pensions

5% — private pensions

15% — from assets: accumulated capital

3% — veterans' benefits

4% — public assistance

1% — contributions from others

2% — all other sources

I have italicized the only items in that list that you can control. If you have some earnings, yes, it is possible to take positive measures to increase them. If you have assets, accumulated capital, that is something else you can control and endeavor to make more productive. Not another item on that list of nine is within your control. Your Social Security probably will be increased as inflation continues. Possibly some of the others will reflect rising living costs to some extent. But, primarily, the battle to keep ahead of rising living costs is *your* battle. It is up to you to take every thoughtfully considered step you can to improve your own situation. Since only 15 percent of the income of the average retired person comes from the capital he or she has accumulated, the effort to keep total income in line with current living costs is immense. It demands that you be willing to change any thoughts, doubts, habits and prejudices that may have become obsolete — that may stand in your path.

What should your capital earn for you in order to combat inflation effectively? Burton Malkiel, Chairman of the Economics Department at Princeton and former member of the President's Council of Economic Advisors, in his book, "The Inflation-Beater's Investment Guide," offers an easy formula. He calls it his "Rule of 72." Using his rule you can determine how long it will take for any given rate of inflation to cut the buying power of your dollars in half. All you do is divide 72 by the inflation rate and you have the answer. If the inflation rate is 12, and you believe it will stay around that figure for a number of years, just divide 72 by 12. The answer is 6. *It will take only 6 years for the value of your dollars to be cut in half.* Disturbing news. But armed with that news you have a great deal of motivation to act. You can see what is coming. Forewarned is forearmed.

It seems evident that the surest way to try to compensate for any rate of inflation is to have after tax income that matches or exceeds it. To find the answer to that one you have another easy formula. If your top

---

*Published by W. W. Norton & Company

bracket for federal income taxes is, for example, 40 percent, you have 60 percent left after Uncle Sam is through with you. Divide the inflation rate by 60 and you have the yield you need. Staying with the 12 percent inflation example...12 percent divided by 60 = one fifth or 20 percent. Sounds impossible to achieve? Have you forgotten about *total return*? That is one possible answer. More to follow.

You are not a statistic. You are a highly individual being. Just because the Social Security Bureau established the fact that the average person at or beyond age 65 has income being produced in the manner you just saw does not mean it is true in your case. But if you are truly human there is an excellent chance that you cannot, at this moment, say what your percentages are. After all, you are not like a corporation with a balance sheet and a financial statement. *Perhaps you should be.*

An income improvement campaign

If you sincerely want to take every sensible measure at your command to deal vigorously with the inflation pinch — if you have a genuine desire to so organize your financial life so that all other aspects of your life can and will remain at the high level you have known and enjoyed, you need a personal financial statement. You need to know what tools you have to employ in your income improvement campaign. You need to know where you are losing. You need to know where you are doing well but might do better.

There's nothing intimidating about the writing of a personal financial statement. The kind of statement you need will have no resemblance to AT&T's or General Motors'. The sole purpose of putting some of your financial facts on paper is to make it easy for you to see what you have, what it is doing for you, what you can control and what you cannot control. Here are the forms to use:

CONTROLLABLE ASSETS

	Current Value	Paying Percentage	Monthly Income in Dollars
Checking Accounts			
Savings in Banks			
Savings in S & L			
Certificates of Deposit			
Money Market Accounts			
Money Market Funds			
Stocks (List each)			
Bonds (List each)			
Mutual Funds (List each)			
Home			
Other Real Estate			
Life Ins. Cash Values			
Business Owned by You			
Other			

TOTAL $ _____ $ _____

UNCONTROLLABLE ASSETS

	Monthly Income in Dollars
Social Security	
Pension	
Profit Sharing Plan	
Annuity	
Other	

TOTAL $

PAYMENTS ON DEBTS

	Percentage of Interest You Buy	Monthly Payments in Dollars
Mortgage		
Bank Loan		
Installment Payments		
(List)		
Other (Do not include rent, utilities or other normal living costs.)		

TOTAL $

TOTAL of both CONTROLLABLE and
UNCONTROLLABLE INCOME $

INCOME IN EXCESS OF
MONTHLY PAYMENTS $

Complete the forms and you have a clear picture of how you look as an operating business. You have a balance sheet that covers everything except your day-to-day living expenditures and the money you spend on pleasure.

To give yourself this important help you may have to phone a few people: your securities and/or real estate broker, the institution holding your mortgage, and your insurance agent. The work involved is not difficult or time consuming. It may prove to be one of the most rewarding things you have ever done.

Once you have it all on paper, study it carefully. There will be things that will fairly leap off the pages. You will see where some of your controllable assets are earning far too little, perhaps nothing. In reviewing any securities, keep in mind that the dividend payments tell only part of the story. *Total return* is what counts. If you are not sure of the facts put your broker to work. Have him tell you what percentage of growth in value your investments have provided in the past 12 months and over the past 5 years. A one year history can be deceptive but a five year history carries some authority. It gives you a firmer base for judging future possibilities. You may discover that some of your investments are giving you a *total loss* instead of a *total return.*

Your uncontrollable assets are nice to look at but that's about all. They really are uncontrollable. What about your debts? They may or may not be within your control. This and many other considerations will be discussed in detail in the chapters to follow. Have your financial statement before you as you read. It will add flesh, blood and bones to a number of the subjects covered. You will have a better grasp of how you can apply ideas that may have strong appeal for you.

Chapter Two

Planning
Ahead

Y ou haven't retired? Perhaps you never
will. You may come to the conclusion that there is no
special appeal to calling a halt to your present occupation...that you have no reason to shift to a new activity...or you may decide that you can't afford to retire.
But even if you have no solid plan to retire and the
organization you work for has no compulsory retirement age, you may have to change your mind. Economic
conditions, a change in company policy, legislation, an
accident or illness can deprive you of the choice.

Statistically, the likelihood is that you *will* retire. At
the close of the last century 68 percent of males 65 years
old or older were still working; 39 percent were still
working in 1954. By 1963 the figure had dropped to 24
percent, and today between 5 and 10 percent still head
for work each weekday morning. For female workers
historic figures are lacking, but current figures appear
to be similar to those for men.

If you have not retired, are planning to retire or aren't sure, you are looking ahead or you wouldn't be reading these words. You are giving yourself an invaluable advantage. The more time you have to prepare for the possibility of retirement the more rewarding and comfortable those years can be.

Two factors make planning ahead particularly important: one is the question of how you will spend the retirement years in terms of mental and physical activity; the second is financial — how well you will be able to maintain your chosen life style. It is difficult to say which of those factors carries the greater weight. Don't underestimate the critical importance of either one. They overlap and intertwine, and the balance will tip to one side or the other in individual cases. Your physical and mental health can be profoundly influenced by what you do with your retirement years — and your ability to do what you want to do may depend totally on your financial resources.

Graduate to retirement

Make your retirement a graduation...a step up rather than a step down. Whatever you want for yourself won't just happen. It must be planned. The evidence is that very few people prepare. The brutal fact is that in this, the wealthiest nation in the world, one out of every six U.S. citizens age 65 or older lives in poverty. What a miserable end to a lifetime of hope and belief that the future would take care of itself. But that kind of blind faith accounts for much of the lack of planning and preparation. Life has simply been too good in this country. Throughout the earning years high pay, wide open credit and the lure of limitless luxuries have blocked all vision of what is waiting when the paycheck stops.

Vast numbers of people believe that Social Security will provide all that is needed to live comfortably...a seriously false assumption. Social Security is an income *supplement.* It never was intended to provide full support. Increases in benefits that attempt to keep the monthly checks in line with rising living costs are wonderful but they don't close the big gap between total need and supplemental help. How important a supplement is depends on where and how you live. James Schultz, Brandeis University economist, expressed it this way, *"Those who rely on Social Security can go from comfortable lives to the ranks of the near poor in a very short time."*

Much dependence has been based on pension plans. All too often they have proven to be a shocking disappointment. There are far too many ifs, ands and buts. When the Employee's Retirement Income Security Act (ERISA) was enacted in 1974, there was general belief that the government had surrounded pension plans with all the needed safeguards. That was the intention of the Congress, but it backfired. The regulations were so tough and so costly for small and medium size companies that tens of thousands of employers discontinued those plans. And even those that remained in force have restrictions as to the number of years an employee must be on the payroll before pension plan benefits are assured. This and other pitfalls can leave employees empty-handed or light-handed at the end of the line.

A firm grasp of the financial needs you will face when you retire depends to a great extent on what you plan to do after you leave your present employment, business or profession. Once you have a clear picture of what you want to do you can reach some conclusions as to the capital or the income you will need.

Assuming that you do not elect to start a new activity, a new venture, or adventure, the generally accepted belief is that you will need about 80 percent of the income you had during your most recent earning years. Stepping into the "senior citizen" category brings with it some economic advantages. Medicare, parts A and B, take care of so many medical costs that it has saved untold numbers of people from financial ruin when serious, prolonged illnesses struck. Transportation, since there is likely to be less of it and because it is often customary to give people over 65 special rates, will cost less. Lunches and clothing requirements generally permit some worthwhile cuts in the budget. Taxes are lower. Starting with your 65th year you may claim an extra exemption when you file your federal income tax return. If you are married and file a joint return and both of you have passed the magic 65 you may claim two extra exemptions. Retirees can also get a retirement income credit of as much as 15 percent. And Social Security income is tax free.

Due to inflation deciding what income you'll need when you retire is only realistic for starters

What must be kept in mind, however, is that even though 80 percent of former earnings may be all you need to continue to live as you have been living, that is only true for starters if inflation continues to be a potent force. For example, a couple with $18,000 of income in the first year of retirement, assuming an average inflation rate of 10 percent a year, would need twice as much — $36,000 — by the time they enter the eighth of their "golden years." That intimidating fact makes the exploration into increasing capital — adding to your flow of dollars for spending *after* retirement — the primary thrust of *The Retirement Money Book.*

Will you have 80 percent of the income you earned before retiring? That is a fairly easy question to answer. Jot down round figures for:

Income from

Social Security .... $	_____
Pension	_____
Savings	_____
Investments	_____
Annuity...........................	_____
Other	_____
TOTAL $	_____

How close does it come to 80 percent of what you are now earning or did earn? (If you don't know what your Social Security income will amount to, get a REQUEST FOR STATEMENT OF EARNINGS postcard from any nearby Social Security Bureau office, or write for one to:

Social Security Administration
P.O. Box 57
Baltimore, Md. 21203

Fill in the few facts required and drop it in the mail. They'll tell you what to expect.

Look at your own income figures and take into account what continuing inflation can do to you. Sure, your Social Security checks may reflect the 10 percent a year increase in living costs. But what about your other income? The next thing to ask is if you have given yourself a big enough base of income-producing capital to make you feel at ease about what lies ahead?

If you have some years between today and the day when present earnings end, *do you feel comfortable about the amount of money you now are putting aside each year?*

Early retirement

Early retirement appeals to many people. The idea is particularly inviting if you are planning on a new career. The new career may be a business venture, the full-time pursuit of a hobby or an absorbing interest in an activity that may produce income or may pay nothing at all — just a determination to steep yourself in something that has powerful appeal for you. If any of these ideas, ambitions, or dreams are to be realized, the younger you are when you make the transition, the greater the likelihood that you will be able to involve yourself with maximum vigor and the longer will be the period when you will be harvesting the rewards.

Early retirement and Social Security

One of the considerations when you engage in a *"should I or shouldn't I"* early retirement debate with yourself is what it will mean in terms of your Social Security income. The facts are these: If you take early retirement at age 62* your basic benefit will be reduced by 20 percent. That amounts to 6 2/3 percent for each of the three years between ages 62 and 65. For example: if the basic benefit you have earned amounts to $432 a month and you retire at age 62, you will get $342.70 a month. Retire at 63 and it will be $374.50. At 64 you'll get $403.30.

The reduction in benefits is permanent

It can be summed up this way using the above example. Retire at 62 and between that time and your 65th birthday you will collect $12,337.20 that you will not receive if you wait to retire at age 65. But it isn't that simple. There are other factors to be weighed. The reduction in your benefits is permanent. Even though you will get whatever cost of living increases come along, they will always be based on your reduced benefits. In addition to that, it is probable that if you wait until you are 65 years old your basic benefit will be greater. Under normal circumstances you will be at the

---

*A widow or widower may take early retirement at age 60.

peak of your earnings. Your basic benefit is determined by taking the average of all of your earnings for a specific number of years. Your top earnings between your 62nd and 65th year will be added at the top and the three years at the low end of the record will come off. Your average earnings will be greater and so will your basic benefit.

If your basic benefit remains unchanged it will take 15 years for the difference between the full and reduced benefits to recapture the $12,337.20 received during the three years used in our example. It will take less time, of course, if your benefits do increase, as they probably will.

In the process of deciding, give serious thought to the longevity tables. Your family history in that connection and the state of your health are of obvious importance.

LIFE EXPECTANCY TABLE

Age	Male	Female
50	24.6	30.5
55	20.7	26.2
60	17.1	22.1
65	14.0	18.4
70	11.1	14.7
75	8.7	11.5
80	6.9	8.9
85	5.5	6.9

U.S. Department of Health and Human Services LIFE EXPECTANCY TABLE based on vital statistics 1978.

Working longer and saving more

Throw on the scale another plus for not retiring early. At that time of life when retirement looms ahead you are particularly aware of what you have and have not accumulated. You are able to see what your savings and investments will be able to provide for you in terms of income. Because, with voluntary or forced retirement just around the corner, these facts achieve vastly increased importance for you. It is quite likely that should you continue working, you will save and invest a far greater percentage of your income than you did in the earlier years. The extra money you manage to save and put to work, in the most effective way you can, will make a great difference in what you will have left to live on when you do retire. Those extra savings would not have been possible had you taken early retirement. They serve, therefore, to somewhat counter-balance the additional Social Security income early retirement affords. However, do not lose sight of the fact that you are comparing taxable income against the tax-free Social Security benefits.

What will you "graduate" to?

Some people are purringly happy doing nothing after they retire. They are relatively rare. The medical profession has concluded that stepping from an active, busy life to complete inactivity can be dangerous to your health. The first few months of not having to get up to the ringing of an alarm clock... not having to be some place on time... not have responsibilities, deadlines or quotas to meet and daily problems to solve... can be fun. Once the novelty wears thin and boredom sets in, however, there isn't much to think about except yourself and how you feel. And if you spend too much of your time worrying about how you feel you won't feel well very long. More to the point, you won't *remain well* very long.

The National Institutes of Health made a study of older people and concluded that those with more complex and varied days lived longer than those who had dull routines. Dr. Leslie S. Libow, a leading geriatric specialist, has stated that retired people today are leading more active lives. *"People now expect more of them-*

selves in retirement, both in the way of physical activity and intellectual challenge," he observed. He pointed out that a good deal of what appears to be senility is actually depression linked to a lifestyle lacking goals and direction.

Older people produce work that equals that of younger workers

Dr. Robert N. Butler, director of the National Institute on Aging, reports that only 5 percent of the elderly population live in nursing homes and other institutions and that the average age of admission is 80.

As to capability, the Department of Labor and the National Council on Aging have concluded studies that show that older persons are able to produce work that in quality and quantity equals that of younger workers.

Jarold Kieffer of the Academy for Educational Development and director of a study on careers of older Americans, has said, *"We're rapidly approaching the time when most workers will automatically enter second careers at retirement simply to remain active and to supplement their pensions."*

Covering all normal possibilities, you have these choices:

A. Find paid employment
B. Start a business of your own for profit
C. Pursue a hobby or skill that may or may not produce a profit but has a good chance of breaking even
D. Devote yourself to something you enjoy doing that pays nothing at all

63 percent of U.S. citizens save too little

Due to current economic pressures there is an increasing need to think about finding employment or operating some kind of enterprise calculated to make money after retirement.

In 1981 The American Council of Life Insurance conducted a survey titled *"Americans and Retirement: The Financial Crisis."* A total of 1,000 working Americans were interviewed, including 437 covered by company pension plans. The conclusion they drew was the *"The average working American, increasingly pressed by inflation and a high tax burden, sees his or her family in a financial bind that threatens their ability to retire.*

"While 63 percent of all Americans feel that they are saving too little, an even higher 72 percent of working Americans feel that their savings for retirement are inadequate. As a result, almost half the work force feel they won't be able to afford to retire."

When asked if they were putting any money aside for retirement, 51 percent said that they were putting no money aside. The combination of that group and those who said that they were saving less than they thought was necessary came to 72 percent. Asked to explain the lack of savings for future needs, an overwhelming 83 percent said that other expenses make saving for retirement difficult.

If you have not retired and have a number of years between today and the time when you may or will retire, do you feel as the 83 percent do? If you do, ask yourself a question: *What would I do if my earnings were cut 10 or 15 percent tomorrow?* The answer has to be that somehow you would manage ... you'd get by. It just might be a good idea, for the retired person you will be some day, to play the part of your employer and to self-impose that 10 or 15 percent cut, taking that part of your earnings and putting it where it can roll up its sleeves and work for you.

How much should you save? This may help. The ideal amount to save is generally considered to be 15 percent of earned income. What will that accomplish for you? Here is a table that provides some answers.

The table below will tell you how many years your savings will last after age 65 if you spend enough each year to equal 80 percent of your earnings at retirement. It is assumed that you will have the money at work earning a uniform 12 percent during the accumulation period.

Your Age	Your present earnings annually		
	$15,000	$20,000	$25,000
50	37 years	19 years	14 years
55	10	7	6
60	3	2	2

The figures do not take into account any other income, such as Social Security, pensions, annuities and investments. The table does, however, give you some basis for measuring the dimensions of your retirement needs and what you should do to deal with the problem.

Looking for employment

Either because you will feel compelled to or will want to, you may decide to look for employment when you leave your current occupation. Help is available. An organization called Forty Plus is one source. There are independent Forty Plus organizations in a number of major cities. Its services are free. Its concentration is to help experienced executives and professionals. To give you an idea of the success of their efforts, here is an excerpt from the Forty Plus of Washington's folder:

"And because the Forty Plus system has been so consistently successful in helping members find new and better paying positions, Forty Plus is now the largest pool of experienced executives and professionals in the Washington area. Which means

that many employers bring their openings to Forty Plus first. Considering this, it shouldn't surprise you to learn that over 2,000 employers use Forty Plus. So do a lot of 'headhunters'. Sometimes companies have sent representatives to Forty Plus meetings and ended up hiring several people."

Forty Plus organizations are located in many large cities including Oakland, California; Toronto, Canada; Denver, Colorado; Washington, D.C.; Honolulu, Hawaii; Chicago, Illinois; New York, New York; Philadelphia, Pennsylvania; Cleveland, Ohio; and Houston, Texas.

If paid employment of any kind is your choice, will there be reason to consider how much capital may be needed to finance it? If the actual or anticipated earnings from employment are a good deal less than you realized before making the change, the difference must come from a pension or an annuity, if you have one, or from the earnings of whatever capital you have accumulated. It is not likely to come from Social Security until you are 72 years old. Until you reach the age of 72 earnings of $6,000 a year or more reduces or eliminates Social Security payments. For every two dollars of earnings beyond $6,000 one dollar is deducted from Social Security payments. $6,000 is the 1981 earnings ceiling. It will increase automatically in succeeding years. The important word is *earnings*. It does not matter how much *unearned income* you receive from sources such as pensions, dividends, interest, royalties, etc. Only earnings resulting from your time and effort count.

Perhaps you can have income exceeding $6,000 without sacrificing Social Security. Here's what Ray Piler did.

Ray Piler and four other architects had a partnership. A condition of the partnership was that when any partner reached the age of 65 he would have to retire so that the remaining partners could admit younger people to the ownership group. Ray knew that his retirement date was coming. He wasn't happy about it but had no choice. He did not want to step into a life without activity and challenge. At the same time he relished the thought of being relieved of the daily pressure of a full and busy schedule and the deadline oriented routine he had lived with for so many years. A year before his crucial birthday he began to look around for a solution and found one. The president of the bank Ray and his firm patronized knew Ray and had a good deal of respect for his experience and knowledge. Ray called on him. He knew that the president was in close touch with the business community. Ray asked for his advice about where he might find appropriate part-time employment.

The president said, "How about working with us, Ray? From time to time we are approached to lend money to exceptionally complex construction projects. The run-of-the-mill cases we can examine and deal with without problem, but when faced with some really big, highly involved situations, we sometimes find it necessary to call on an outside specialist who, for a fee, analyzes the project and gives us the facts we need. You certainly are equipped to do that kind of work. What would you think about coming on board as an outside consultant? We'll pay you $1,000 a month and the chances are we would not put you to work more than three or four times a year."

Ray Piler took a few days to think that one over. And he did some digging. The fact that $12,000 was well below his earnings as an active architect didn't disturb him because he had prepared for this transition over the years. He had been paying regular sums into an annuity contract. Over a period of time his total investment in the contract had amounted to $80,000. Thanks to compounding on a tax deferred basis, which annuities make possible, the earnings had added $72,000 to the account, for a total of $152,000. What concerned Ray most was that the Social Security income he and his wife could realize came to almost $8,000 a year and it would be tax-free. If he accepted the bank's offer he would lose all of the Social Security income for the next seven years and $12,000, after taxes, would net less than $8,000 tax-free.

But Ray found a way to have his cake and eat it... a la mode. He went back to his friend, the bank president, and said, "John, I appreciate your offer and I want to accept it but on slightly different terms. You told me that you anticipated needing my services just three or four times a year. Pay me the $1,000 a month that you offered... but not as a consultant. Pay that monthly fee for my agreement to make myself available when needed."

That caused the bank president to blink a bit. "How does that make a difference?"

"It makes a great difference," Ray said. "Social Security regulations bar me from any benefits if I earn $6,000 or more per year. During the months when I stand-by but perform no services for you, the fees you pay me will not represent earnings. When I work, putting in time for four months of the year, my total reportable earnings are confined to the $1,000 I *earn* in each of those four months, and that is all. I retain $8,000 a year in tax-free income from Social Security."

The bank president understood and accepted the *stand-by* idea. Ray was still going to be well under his customary annual income even when he combined the $12,000 from the bank and the $8,000 from Social Security. His final step was to put his annuity accumulation to work.

There are three basic types of annuity contracts. There is the immediate annuity where you pay in a substantial sum and start drawing annuity payments right away; the deferred annuity, where you make the one big payment but postpone the time when you will start taking monthly checks; the accumulation annuity, such as Ray Piler's, where you pay into the account on a systematic basis over a period of years and then, at some later date, you start drawing.

There are two parts to the deferred and accumulation annuities. The first part is the period before the monthly pay-outs and the second occurs when pay-outs begin. The shift from part one to part two is called *annuitizing*. Until the contract is annuitized the owner may withdraw any part of what is in the account. After it is annuitized, the monthly payments, based on the terms of the contract, become frozen. The contract owner cannot draw anything more.

Ray Piler's annuity had not been annuitized. He still had control. The $72,000 in the account that had accumulated tax-free, and the $80,000 he had put in out of his own pocket are regarded, from a tax standpoint, as two separate entities. Ray was free to draw on the account in any way he pleased and *until he had withdrawn the entire $80,000 he had put in, his withdrawals would be free of taxes.* This was his own money on which he had paid taxes. It had come out of his regular income *after* the payment of taxes. He would not be required to pay taxes on it a second time. It is regarded as return of capital. When he goes beyond the $80,000 and starts taking the earnings which had been tax sheltered over the years, those withdrawals would be taxable.

The decision Ray made was to draw $11,000 a year from his annuity until his 72nd birthday. This would accomplish two important things for him. First, the account, less his withdrawals, would continue to earn income that would not be subject to current taxation. Those tax-sheltered earnings would remain in the account. Second, since his withdrawals would not exceed his own investment, they would be untaxed.

Time enough, he figured, to decide on the next step when he reached age 72. At that point he may decide to annuitize his contract, continue to take withdrawals, or take all the money in the account and invest it where it might earn a greater return. When he does take out the full amount, or monthly withdrawals, he will be subject to taxes. But, he reasoned, at 72 he might want to stop working altogether. He would be in a still lower tax bracket, reducing the portion he had to pay to Uncle Sam.

There are various kinds of annuity contracts. They are explained in detail in the next chapter.

Establishing a venture for profit

Putting yourself in an activity with the objective of earning money can be something very small, making minimal demands on your time and effort and requiring little or no capital, or it can be a fully absorbing, substantial project calling for substantial financing.

Your economic situation will be the principal deciding factor. If you have no reason to be concerned about there being enough income to support your way of life and you elect to pursue an interest and to make some money at the same time that can be a gratifying avenue to follow. Keep it small. Keep your original objectives in mind: you want a small business that will keep you active, interested, happy and give you some extra income. You are not attempting to build an expanding business requiring constant investment of profits. Don't let easy and early indications of success propel you into too rapid a build-up, with sizeable investments of capital and increasing self involvement.

Going a step beyond the choice of a relaxed, part-time way of cashing in on a hobby — the next level is a full-time enterprise. More often than not this takes the form of a retail business, a business frequently operated by man and wife and requiring no other personnel.

Before taking the first step, sit down and answer some questions. A husband and wife should deal with the questions together.

- Do you really know enough about the business being considered?
- Have you studied the degree of interest and/or demand for what you plan to offer?
- How well can you compete with those already established in the same field?
- Are those in the same field prospering?
- How much capital will it take?
- Have you made realistic income and cost projections?
- Are you able to put more money into it if your projections prove to be overly optimistic?
- Have you taken your plans and projections to experienced, knowledgeable people who know this type of business?
- Will suppliers give you credit?
- Have you located a logical location?
- Have you done a study of the traffic flow, parking facilities, customer and business safety at the location?
- What happens if you become ill or disabled?
- Have you chosen an enterprise you will enjoy?

If you face up to each of these questions and are confident that you are on the right track, hold off until you have gathered all the guidance and help you can get. The counsel of your lawyer, accountant, insurance agent, real estate agent and others can be invaluable, provided that you get their ideas before you have committed yourself to anything.

Draw on the free help you can get from Washington. The Small Business Administration has an amazing wealth of practical aids. As an example, they have a booklet, *SMA 71, Checklist for Going into Business* that is exceptionally thorough. It encompasses ideas that can make extreme differences in your thinking and your actions. Send for it and ask for their long list of publications. You will find several others that address themselves to the nature of the enterprise you are contemplating. Write to:

Small Business Administration
1441 L Street, N.W.
Washington, D.C. 20005

or to:

Small Business Administration
P.O. Box 15434
Fort Worth, Texas 76119

or check your phone book to see if SBA has a branch located near you.

Another invaluable source of help is from a trade association if the type of business you are interested in has one. The chances are that it does. There are several thousand trade associations. If you don't know the name or location of a trade association in your field write to:

American Society of Association Executives
1575 Eye Street, N.W.
Washington, D.C. 20005

Buying an existing business may be far better than starting from scratch. A brand new business demands the expenditure of a certain amount of money before you open and that may be the smallest part of your capital needs. The investment never stops there. Inevitably there are mistakes to be corrected, promotional costs, new or added equipment and a sizeable amount must be budgeted for the unexpected. Buying an established business can eliminate much of that expense. It is established. Customers are in the habit of dealing there. Time and experience have taken care of the corrections that had to be made, the items that had to be added.

It is not at all unusual to be able to buy a going, successful business for little money. If the owner wants to retire, is in ill health, wants to move on to other interests, has passed away and the business is being sold by an estate, it is quite possible that a business can be bought on terms with a modest down payment. It is well worth investigation.

Look for projects that require little capital

Low capital needs is a very desirable factor. A business based on services does not require machinery, equipment or inventory. Your own experience and training may suggest the type of service business you can offer. A personnel manager should do well with the operation of an employment agency. Coming from an engineering or mechanical background, various types of repair businesses suggest themselves. Teaching can lead to the establishment of a training business. And so on.

Open your mind to franchises. Going into a business of your own has plusses and minuses. Some of the most threatening minuses are the elements of chance and the unknown. A new enterprise, starting from base zero, has to feel its way, developing direction, policy, image and public acceptance slowly and not at all surely.

The Small Business Administration estimates that 81 percent of all businesses fail within five years. In vivid contrast to those intimidating figures, the Department of Commerce reports that in each year since 1971 less than 5 percent of *franchise-owned* businesses were discontinued. In 1979, the last year for which actual data are available, only 3.8 percent of franchise-owned outlets dropped out, and many of them for reasons other than financial failure.

At the beginning of the 1980s roughly one-third of all retail sales in the United States were via franchises, accounting for close to 350 billion dollars in sales, produced by approximately 367,000 franchise-owned outlets.

The reasons why the franchise method of going into business has such an overwhelmingly greater success record are not hard to pinpoint. When you start a new enterprise via a franchise you are taking a success pattern and duplicating it. You have the backing of an organization that has been through the trials and errors of new business. It has rooted out the errors and built upon the things that worked. In more cases than not, you have a product or service that is known to the public and you have the support of national and local advertising. One of the most valuable plusses you have is that you go into your business venture having been guided and trained by an ally who understands the business thoroughly and has strong motivation to want to see you do well. The average franchise involves a continuing relationship between you and the franchisor. This is not a situation where you buy something and the seller walks away, The ongoing relationship may be in terms of an annual fee, a percentage of sales going to the franchisor, the purchase of equipment, goods and supplies, or similar arrangements. The better you do, the better the parent company does. In addition to that, the franchising company is seriously hurt by any failures for they damage their efforts to attract other franchisees as well as the reputation of their product or service.

It requires less capital to start a franchise operation than it takes to open a business that is totally independent. The avoidance of costly errors and miscalculations, alone, can account for significant savings. The costs of establishing an accounting system, printed needs, displays, advertising and scores of other things can add up to considerable sums when starting from the ground up, but when these elements have been developed and proven they are bought in large quantities. The costs for each participant can reflect great savings.

There is a general impression that a franchise operation is almost confined to the fast-food business since these are the best known and the most visible franchise operations. The fact is that there are 1,500 or more companies offering franchises and there are few types of business not embraced by the franchise method. In recent years there has been increasing franchise activity in such fields as printing, copying, real estate, employment, educational services and products, health care, insurance, computer products and services, beauty and health aids, etc. The businesses involved range from the function of a single individual working out of his or her home to the ownership and operation of large motels and hotels.

The International Franchise Association, a trade association for franchisors, publishes a directory listing hundreds of franchisors, itemizing the kind of business each is in and, in many cases, the number of outlets now operating, the cash investment required, what is offered in return for that investment and stating the required qualifications of applicants. For information about availability of the directory write to:

International Franchise Association
Suite 1005, 1025 Connecticut Avenue
Washington, D.C. 20036

What type of franchise is right for you? One of the real advantages of entering a new business via the franchise route is that you will have a relatively accurate idea of the amount of capital you will need. You will learn what the initial investment will be and will be told what to anticipate in terms of ongoing outlays, what level of income can be expected and about how long it will take before you start showing a profit. The first question, therefore — is this a venture you can afford — is more readily answered when your election is a franchise. Initial fees vary from zero — you pay a percentage of sales — to millions for franchises for Hilton and Holiday Inns and other businesses of that magnitude.

But there are many other questions of extreme importance.

- Are you suited, from a health standpoint, experience, education and the ability to learn and hold on to new concepts?
- Does the type of business you are looking at match you — your interests, temperament, the number of hours you are willing and able to devote to the development and management of the business? Is your personality in keeping with the type of business?
- As a married couple do the two of you see eye to eye on the project?
- Are you genuinely enthused about the nature of the business you will be spending your time in?
- Are you good at managing others?

Many other questions will pose themselves as you investigate one or more franchise possibilities. While the bulk of the questions must be answered by you, there are other questions you should bring to your lawyer. There are some franchises that may be handled by you strictly as an investment. You hire others to do the work involved. This is not always permitted by franchisors but if it suits your thinking, it can be an interesting idea to pursue.

And, of course, there are negatives. As is sometimes true in any type of business, there are shady characters and shady deals. Organizations such as the International Franchise Association, which has a rigid code of ethics, tries to police its membership. Some fifteen states require franchisors to register and to file complete registration statements. The Federal Trade Commission has an established *Franchise Rule*. The rule is a federal law. It requires that every franchisor prepare an extensive document and give a copy to any prospective purchaser before he or she buys a franchise. Within the disclosure statement there are at least twenty different categories of information about the franchise: required fees, basic investment, bankruptcy and litigation history of the company, how long the franchise will be in effect, an audited financial statement of the franchisor, substantiation of earnings claims and more.

If you send a check for $8.50 to the Superintendent of Documents, Government Printing Office, Washington, D.C. 20402, they will provide you with the *Franchise Opportunities Handbook*. This Department of Commerce publication lists over 850 franchise companies and what each offers. If you see any that hold special interest for you, write to them and ask for their disclosure documents. The surest way to protect yourself from bad deals, whether they be bad because of dishonesty or poor management, is to locate and talk with people who have chosen and are operating the franchise you are investigating. Beyond that there are a number of things you should be sure to learn before taking action.

- Is the product or service in demand throughout the year or is it seasonal?
- Is it sound business for your particular area?
- How long has it been on the market?
- Is it a faddish business that might quickly fade away?
- How strong and reliable is the parent company?
- How prompt are their deliveries?
- How do they stack up with their competition?
- Are there governmental standards involved? Does this create any problems?
- How realistic are the profit projections? Have you had them reviewed by an accountant — by people who know the business?

- How detailed is the franchise agreement as to what you will get for the fee? Does it include training, travel to the training center, living expenses while there? Does it cover national advertising or will you pay a prorated share? Does it include any local advertising? Is centralized bookkeeping involved and is it covered by the fee? What does the fee give you in supplies, equipment, fixtures, display, inventory, etc. The fact that the fee may not cover all of the above does not mean that anything is wrong, but it is vital for you to have a completely detailed accounting of all current and future expenses.
- What terms are available? Is any part of the fee refundable? To what extent are you legally obligated to pay future fees and/or royalties or commissions?
- What continuing services can you rely on and at what cost, if any?
- On top of the fee, are you required to buy any equipment, furnishings or anything else? How competitive are those charges? May you buy from other sources?
- How many of your people will be trained? Will future employees be trained? Where? What are the costs?
- Will you be given sound assistance in choosing the right kind of location, and guidance on the lease?
- Are you protected as to territory? Can the territory be changed without your consent?
- What happens if you choose not to renew? Do you have the right to sell your franchise?

A few facts supplied by the International Franchise Association are reassuring:

- Of 15,364 franchise contracts up for renewal in 1979, 92 percent were renewed.

- There were 367,207 franchise-owned outlets in 1979 and only 7,480 agreements were terminated ...2 percent.
- 99 percent of franchisees who requested permission to sell their franchises were permitted to do so.

The profitable pursuit of your craft and hobby skills

Because this is *The Retirement Money Book*, the concentration is on ways to have more money in the retirement years. For that reason the intriguing world of activities that pay nothing, but can make the retired years richly rewarding in other ways, will not be covered. There are, however, vast opportunities to devote your new life to the profitable pursuit of hobbies and skills at which you excel and which you enjoy. A ready-made avenue to earnings from things you create with your hands is a fascinating nonprofit organization called *The Elder Craftsmen, Inc.*

Established in 1955, the *Elder Craftsmen* was organized and has been developed and expanded expressly to help people aged 60 or more to market handicrafts. It is headquartered in New York City but it retails the products of people from all over the United States and Canada. In addition, its activities have attracted so much national attention that others have picked up the idea and have put together similar groups in many places. As the *Elder Craftsmen* expresses it, *"Since 1955, Elder Craftsmen has been working to bring older people a whole new world of opportunity through crafts... opportunity for personal fulfillment, opportunity to supplement income and opportunity to find release from physical or mental hardship. All at the very time it is working to nurture the American craft tradition."*

The craftsmen who create the items retailed by *Elder Craftsmen* work in several ways. The items they make are sold on consignment and the individual craftsman gets 60 percent of the retail price. The balance goes to help maintain the store and other costs of operation. That is an exceptionally generous arrangement. Some craftspeople produce merchandise on assignment. These may be items made to some buyer's special instructions. A third category is handled by the *Elder Craftsmen Controlled Production Unit.* This is available to the same age group — 60 or older — who have demonstrated special skills and want help in procuring quality materials and supplies. The CPU furnishes the supplies and the craftspeople get 50 percent of the selling price. In addition to all of this, those fortunate enough to live in the New York City area and who belong to organized senior groups can attend training sessions where their natural skills are developed. They also learn how to teach the craft to other older people. If this means of boosting your income appeals to you there are several steps you can take.

Elder Craftsmen is highly selective in what it offers to the public. They have a reputation for carrying only top quality craftsmanship. Every Thursday, at their main offices at 135 East 65th Street in New York City 10021, craftspeople come with the things they make. These are studied by a knowledgeable committee who make the final selections. Those who cannot come to New York may submit their offerings by shipping them by UPS or parcel post.* Here are your choices:

1. If you have items to offer and are in or near New York City just show up with your samples any

---

*If accepted and sold, the item earns its creator a percentage of its sale price; the balance goes toward paying the group's operating expenses. If the item is not accepted, it is returned with suggestions on how to make it more marketable.

Thursday between 11 a.m. and 3 p.m.. No appointment is needed. *Elder Craftsmen*, 135 East 65th St., New York, N.Y. 10021.

2. If you want to ship your samples address them to the above address.
3. If you want information about the CPU (Controlled Production Unit) program see, write to or phone: Kayla Gluck, same address as above. Telephone — (212) 861-3294.
4. If you want to know if there is a like organization near you, or desire further information about any aspect of the programs, write to: Mrs. Barbara B. Stires, Executive Director, at the 65th Street address, or phone her at (212) 861-5260. If you write, be sure to enclose a stamped envelope addressed to yourself.
5. If you want to visit the retail shop it is located at 850 Lexington Avenue, New York City. The types of handicrafts *Elder Craftsmen* customarily handles includes knitting, crocheting, weaving, needlepoint, quilting, children's clothes, toys, enamel, pottery, leather, woodworking, macrame, seasonal decorations, etc.

Barter can supplement your income

In the previous chapter the subject of barter was mentioned. Barter does not produce income but it is a highly effective way to give yourself more money to spend because it enables you to provide yourself with various goods and services that, otherwise, would call for cash expenditures.

Barter can range from, "If you'll fix my sink, I'll tune your piano," to, "I'll exchange my apartment house for your office building." And there are a thousand variations in between. Not only does the use of barter give you more money for other things it is inflation-proof.

Since becoming interested in the subject and doing some probing I have come across a variety of examples of barter at work. There's the retired accountant who called on a number of restaurants he and his wife like until he found one that gladly made a deal with him. He now handles their books and taxes and he and his wife take many of their meals there. A lady who was a skilled seamstress now gets the dresses and suits she needs by doing alteration work for a smart dress shop. A former owner of a repair garage keeps a local grocer's two trucks and private car in tip-top shape and carries home just about all the groceries he and his wife need.

My favorite is a lady artist who reports that she has had legal services, three new fenders on her car and optical services in exchange for some of her oil paintings. What intrigued me was her need for legal services, fenders *and* optical services. It tells a story. The point is, everyone has something to contribute . . . something that is needed by others. If you like to drive your car — if you love being with little children — if you enjoy reading and/or writing — if you find research interesting — if you are good in the garden — if you have fun talking to people on the telephone — if you get a kick out of meeting people, each of these is a skill that is exchangable for things you need or want. You can do the things you love to do and give yourself extra spending money at the same time, because you are buying with services and not with cash.

Internal Revenue keeps an eye on barter. But their real interest is barter that involves major value exchanges, as in real estate and the like. Exchanges of that magnitude must be reported. But baby sitting in exchange for fresh produce is not the type of barter likely to call for IRS scrutiny.

There exist throughout the United States many non-profit community barter centers. You can join up by making a voluntary contribution of a few dollars, list the skills you have to offer and what you would like in exchange. The center matches up both sides, saving you the task of locating those who you can swap with. These non-profit centers are tax-exempt and IRS is not concerned with them or with the activities of the members.

If you want to learn if there is a barter center in your area and you don't find such a listing in the phone book free information is available. Write to:

Mr. David Tobin
Barter Project
Suite 500, 1111 19th Street
Roslyn, Virginia 22209

or to:

Skills Bank
340 Pioneer Street
Ashland, Oregon 97520

These are both non-profit centers of barter information and will gladly cooperate with you. If you fail to locate a center near you ask these organizations what steps you might take to start one. That could be an exciting, rewarding retirement occupation.

Chapter Three

Cutting Taxes and Increasing Capital

Building capital, enlarging the source of future income

These are subjects with special appeal for those not yet retired. But if you have stepped up to retirement and your major interest is more income, some of the ideas in this chapter will still be valuable to you. If you are retired, have ample income and some to spare, the concepts that follow offer weapons for the battle against continuing inflation — actions to consider if you are planning on something in the future that calls for substantial financing.

Inflation is a personal affair

Whether retired or planning for retirement, inflation is very much in the picture — but the picture may not be as bad as you think.

Inflation is not the same for everyone. It all depends on where your dollars go. Take a few examples. When the government announces the overall rate of inflation, one big factor that enters the calculations is housing. Everyone knows how brutally housing costs have been increasing. But what about you? Housing costs may have increased by as much as 15 percent last year but if you are making mortgage payments which do not change, if you own your home free and clear, if you are a renter and your rent wasn't increased, your increase was ZERO. Utilities: the jumps in the costs of fuel oil, electricity and natural gas have been staggering. For low income people the impact, percentage wise, can mean that their personal inflation rate greatly exceeded the national figure. The more income you have the lower the impact.

What were the biggest leaps in food prices during the past year? If it happened to be beef and shell fish and you have cut down on or never were a big consumer of beef and shellfish, your inflation rate is under par. Even if you are a big beef eater, the impact on you relates to what portion of your income flows to the supermarket. Transportation is another biggie. So are education and medical care. Since you are at the age when you are interested in the money problems of retirement you probably are not paying for anyone's education. If you are covered by Medicare the costs of medical care may not be a sizeable item in your budget. The same goes for transportation.

In your efforts to accumulate capital or to make your capital grow there are two approaches that have particular significance for those who are near to or are in retirement:

1. Steps calculated to avoid, reduce or postpone taxes so that you can maximize the accumulation and building process;
2. Ways to enable your money to grow without exposing it to undue risk.

Taxes will blunt anything you do when you try to increase your capital or income. There are legitimate, ethical ways to sidestep them entirely, to make them smaller or to defer them. Senator Williams of Mississippi, former chairman of the Senate Finance Committee, expressed it well, *"There's nothing that says that a man has to take a toll bridge across a river when there is a free bridge nearby."*

While getting rid of taxes altogether is ideal, and reducing your tax liability is to be welcomed, deferring taxes is also quite rewarding. When the rules and regulations permit you to delay the payment of taxes on income or profits until some time in the future, it is exactly the same as your getting an interest-free loan. For whatever period you enjoy that tax shelter you have money at work, earning dividends, interest or potential profits — money that, under other circumstances, would have gone to the tax collector. That is a tremendous advantage. Therefore, steps calculated to avoid, reduce or postpone taxes are of genuine importance to you.

Putting your money where it can grow without exposing it to undue risk clearly is a must in the capital building process. *Risk* is a much misunderstood word. Many people say that they will not put any of their hard earned dollars at risk. That is impossible. Money is exposed to the risk of loss no matter where it is, no matter what you do with it. The only real value money has is that it can be exchanged for goods and services. In itself it is worth nothing at all. Put money in a tin box and bury it in the back yard. Take it out one, five or ten years later and *if it won't buy as much as when you buried it* you have had a loss. When you buried it you took the risk that it might have more or less buying power when you dug it up. And you lost. There is nothing in this world that guarantees the future buying power of your dollars. Everyone has that risk.

When you put your money someplace where it may earn income or may grow, you are taking a risk. The income may or may not be sufficient to match or exceed rising prices. You may realize the hope for growth, or the opposite can happen. The growth might not be enough to keep you ahead of the buying power game. There may be no growth at all. You could end up with fewer dollars. Whatever can go up can come down. What it boils down to is this: there is a risk of loss when money sits still because buying power does not sit still. It constantly changes. Money thoughtfully put to work, where it has a chance to grow and to earn, also is at risk. The careful person wanting growth and little risk looks for places where the chances of good growth and/or earnings appear to be good and where the possibilities of getting back fewer dollars appear to be small.

Most things in life balance out. The blind man hears better. The deaf are keener observers. Investing money where there is a chance of super profits is balanced by the possibility of equally super losses. Young people may, with reason, take on big risks hoping for big rewards. If they lose, they have plenty of time to accumulate more capital. Older people don't have that luxury of time. People with considerable wealth are able to enter into ventures with sizeable risk-reward potential for they won't be seriously hurt if they lose. The man or woman past age 50 who doesn't have great wealth must treat capital with respect. The risks they take should be modest.

There are a vast number of ways of putting money to work. Since the two steps that are so desirable are the avoidance of taxes and the pursuit of capital growth without undue risk, let's first examine some moves that combine both.

Annuities as a source of lifelong income
In the previous chapter you saw a brief story about one

type of annuity. There is a lot more to tell. An annuity is a contract between a life insurance company and you. As is true of all contracts, the terms can be extremely elastic. Because a life insurance company is involved does not mean that this is a form of life insurance. It isn't. Actually, life insurance really is death insurance since its fundamental purpose is to pay survivors after the insured person dies. An annuity is the opposite. Its fundamental purpose is to pay you money *until* you die.

Single Pay Deferred Fixed Annuity. This is the granddaddy the oldest type of annuity contract. You pay the insurance company a certain amount of money. Most companies require that it be $5,000 or more. You may, of course, increase your investment at any time prior to the start of annuity pay-outs. The company guarantees that when you reach an age of your own choice they will send you checks for a fixed amount for as long as you live. There are other options you may elect which you will read about in a moment. Until the date when the account is annuitized the dollars you invested are guaranteed and will be earning interest in an amount guaranteed by the company. The interest to be paid will differ from company to company but 8 or 9 percent interest guaranteed for the first three to five years is not uncommon. After that the interest will be in harmony with prevailing market rates, which is fair to both you and the company. Your earnings and the interest compounding on those earnings are tax-deferred. There is that interest-free loan mentioned earlier. Your money will be compounding on that tax-favored basis until the time when the contract is annuitized.

Until the contract is annuitized you are free to draw money out. If you do that during the early years, the insurance company will exact some charge, but after the third year generally there is no charge. Until you draw out more than you first put in no taxes are payable on what you withdraw. The annuitizing occurs on a date you name. You don't have to let the account annuitize ever. If you choose, you can take all of your money out. At that time, or whenever you draw in excess of your original investment, taxes become payable. Taxes are paid on the tax-sheltered portions of the annuity payments in the years you receive them. The more you take out the smaller the eventual pay-outs will be. You can bring it to the point where the contract will be cancelled.

When the contract is annuitized the company determines the amount of the monthly check you are to receive. The formula used takes into account various factors including your age, the amount of your original investment plus the compounded earnings and which of several payout options you choose. These are the options offered by most companies:

Single life: For as long as you live you will receive a check each month for an unchanging sum of money. This option pays the maximum amount.

Joint and Survivor: The company will make monthly payments for as long as either of two people live. Generally this covers a husband and wife but it could cover the annuitant and another designated person. Both ages are considered when the amount of the monthly payouts is determined.

Life and Installments Certain: The *certain* period is usually ten or twenty years. This provides that should you die prior to the *certain* period, payments will continue to be paid to your beneficiary for the specified number of years.

Cash Refund Annuity: If you die before everything you invested has been paid out, the remainder of the money will be paid in monthly installments or in a lump sum to your beneficiary.

In each option the company pays nothing beyond the agreed term . . . after you die in the Single Life option . . .

after both lives have ended in the Joint and Survivor option ... after the Installment period or when you die, whichever comes later, and after the full Cash Refund or when you die, whichever comes later. Nothing beyond the terms of the contract is paid to your estate. On the other hand, you can live to be the oldest person in Guinness' book of records and those monthly payments will keep on coming.

All types of annuity contracts have most of these provisions but here are the models from which you may choose:

Accumulation Deferred Annuity. Instead of paying a lump sum you enter into an agreement to make regular payments at regular intervals for a minimum period of time.

Single Pay Immediate Annuity. You pay a sum of money to the insurance company and start receiving the annuity payments right away. Since there is no period of time prior to the contract being annuitized, this bypasses the tax-sheltering of earnings. Some people buy this contract upon receiving a sizeable amount of money from one source or another, and they want the peace of mind of knowing that they will have a check coming in every month, no matter how long they live.

Variable Annuity. This is the insurance companies' answer to the inroads inflation made on fixed annuity sales. The big difference between the fixed and the variable annuity is who takes the investment risk. When a fixed annuity contract is annuitized, the company commits itself to the fixed monthly sum of money it will pay you for life. The company has money invested in a number of income producing securities and expects that their investments will produce sufficient income to take care of the payments to annuitants and give the insurance company a profit. With a variable annuity the company guarantees to pay you an *unchanging percentage of the value of an unchanging number of investment units.* You are taking the risk as to what may happen to the value of those units. The units are almost the same as shares of a mutual fund. In some cases they actually are the shares of a mutual fund. You will see more about that in the next type of annuity. From your standpoint the risk you are taking is not an *undue risk.* Insurance companies are conservative investors. Your units represent money invested in scores of high quality issues — blue chip stocks. The chances are that your units will increase in value in most years and that your income will keep in step with rising living costs or move in front of them. There undoubtedly will be some years when the value of your units will go down and so will your monthly checks. The likelihood is that this will not happen often. Since we have been living with inflation, without a single exception since 1954, the variable annuity seems to make more sense than the fixed annuity.

Wrap-Around Annuity. Some call them *Switch-Fund Annuities.* In this relatively new product you have the joining of a life insurance company and a mutual fund organization managing several mutual funds with different goals and different investment policies. The insurance company provides the annuity contract and the mutual fund company provides the investments. You have the valuable freedom to specify which of the mutual funds you want your annuity *wrapped around.*

For example, you buy a contract for a Deferred Single Pay Variable Annuity. The family of funds managed by the mutual fund organization has, among others, a money market fund. At the time you enter into the contract the money market fund is yielding 15 percent and that is what you elect for your investment. A few years later you have strong reason to believe that common stock values are going to have a dramatic rise. You write a letter instructing a shift from the money market fund to the mutual fund organization's fund concentrating on *growth stocks*. That change is made immediately and you pay nothing for it. Some years after that you retire and make a decision that, once again, income is more important to you than growth. You write another letter and another cost free change is made. You can do that as often as you please until you annuitize, and most companies allow you to make changes once a year thereafter. With the Wrap-Around Variable Annuity, therefore, you have the tax shelter, the opportunity to build your account with high income and the privilege of dictating the nature of the investment as you see fit. The Wrap-Around has the further advantage of giving you the mutual fund investment without sales charge. It is a most attractive package. One problem looms on the horizon at this writing. The package is so attractive and has won so many followers that the government has initiated some activity to do away with the tax deferral. So far this has not happened and there is a good chance that it will not. Check it out before you invest.

An investment dealer will be the right person to see for the Wrap-Around Annuity; for the others as well. Your insurance agent can offer you any except the Wrap-Around.

Annuities — any of the models — can make a lot of sense if you have enough years before retirement to get meaningful benefit from the ability to compound earnings under the tax shelter. After retirement is no time to start unless you have all the income you need that won't be seriously reduced if you apply a block of capital to an annuity. Should you be in that happy situation a

NOTE: At this writing IRS has just issued a restrictive ruling concerning the Wrap-Around Annuity. Some restructuring of the offerings will have to take place. Having discussed this with a number of industry leaders and involved attorneys I find universal conviction that whatever restructuring will occur will not eliminate any of the broad benefits. Check with your broker or financial planner.

variable annuity contract can be your long-term defense against continuing high inflation or the way to build a bigger estate for your heirs.

If you have had a deferred annuity, the time when you retire calls for a decision. Is there a serious need for an income supplement? No two ways about it...that is the time to annuitize...*unless*. There are at least two exceptions. If you learn that the monthly check you'll get will not compare well with a yield you can get elsewhere, take your money, pay the tax, and put your money where it can do a better job for you. If you are uncertain about what the payments will be, ask. The company, broker or insurance agent can and will tell you. The other exception is based on your age and health. If you have put off retiring until you are in your eighties, for example, or if you have reason to believe that you, or you and spouse, don't have too many years to look forward to, any type of annuity payout is a poor bet. Unless you elect to take the ten or twenty year certain option, the company will pay nothing to anyone when you are gone. The ten or twenty year certain option provides some protection against that, but remember that the monthly payments you will receive for as long as you live will be materially less because of that option choice. Get all the figures and see what looks best for you.

At retirement, if you are not in need of the income, do not annuitize. The longer you can enjoy the tax shelter the better off you are. The tax shelter ends when annuity payouts begin.

Retirement plans

Retirement plans qualified by the Internal Revenue Service give you another way of combining tax relief and capital growth. If you are employed by a corporation, perhaps you participate in a pension or profit-sharing plan. Fine if you do. But unless you are a major stockholder, or a top executive, the chances are that you have no control over how the money is invested. As a matter of fact, you can't be sure that you will ever see any of the contributions credited against your name. That all depends on the terms of the plan, how long you will be with the company and other uncertainties. Because of your inability to shape such plans to your own ideas and needs, we will concentrate on retirement plans you may or can control.

Keogh Plan. You may establish a Koegh Plan if you operate a business or profession of your own and have not incorporated. You can be an artist, barber, concert pianist, a cab driver... it doesn't matter. If you earn income by doing what you do, and are not incorporated, this is your opportunity to establish a retirement plan of your own. Having a Keogh Plan allows you to put away up to $15,000 a year, or 15 percent of your earnings, whichever is less. You pay no current federal income taxes on that money. The money will be earning dividends or interest and those earnings also escape taxation for the life of the plan. There is a stipulation. If you employ any people who have been working for you for three or more years, you have to do for them whatever you do for yourself. That does not mean that you are required to pay into their plans as much *money* as you direct to your own plan. It means that the *percentage of compensation* used to determine the contributions must be the same. Say that you earn $150,000 a year. Since you may not contribute more than $15,000 to your own Keogh, the $15,000 you put in represents just 10 percent of your earnings. Therefore, you have to contribute 10 percent of Sally's $15,000 salary, or $1,500 ... 10 percent of George's $38,000, or $3,800 ... and so on.

Not only do you have that very nice tax shelter that is going to have such a beneficial impact on the total that will be waiting for you in the future, you also have an immediate tax saving — two in fact. First, you save taxes on the contributions you make for yourself and for your employees — they are deductible as business expense. Second, those deductions from your taxable income probably put you in a lower tax bracket.

You can put additional money in your Keogh Plan if you have one or more employees covered and at least one of them decides that he or she would like to put aside more by making *voluntary contributions* on his or her own. Under those circumstances you, too, may make extra payments to your own account. Voluntary contributions may be the lesser of $2,500 a year or 10 percent of earnings. One important difference between these and the regular contributions — they are not deductible from taxable income. What the voluntary additions earn, however, is deductible. It is a desirable plus. IRS puts *do not touch* signs on the money in Keogh accounts until you are age 59½, become permanently disabled or die. At age 70½ you must start taking the money out. If you get in a severe financial pinch you may withdraw the money, but taxes become payable that year and, in addition, there is 10 percent penalty. There is no problem with voluntary sums that you may have put in. Take them at any time — but not whatever they earned. When your money does come out of the account in the permitted manner, that is tax time. You can direct the custodian to send you monthly checks, giving you a flow of income over a period of years. If you take that method, you will pay your normal income tax on the total withdrawn each year. The chances are that you will have retired at that time, putting you in a lower bracket and thereby reducing your tax cost.

If you elect to take the entire amount in the plan in a single payment, it becomes a bit involved. If your accumulation amounts to $20,000 or less, half of it is tax free — a $10,000 exemption. If it is between $20,000 and $70,000 you take 20 percent of the amount between $20,000 and the top limit of $70,000, subtract that from your $10,000 exemption and the result is the amount you are permitted to deduct. You pay your regular tax on the rest. Here's how it works:

- Your payout amounts to $50,000
- On the first $20,000 you get a $10,000 exemption
- 20 percent of the remaining $30,000 = $6,000
- Subtract $6,000 from the $10,000 which leaves $4,000; the total exemption you may take.
- You pay tax on $46,000

On to the next step. If your payout is more than $70,000, IRS says you may use the *10-year averaging rule*, sharply reducing what you pay to IRS. Here is how *10-year averaging* works:

You divide the total payout by 10. You then see what a single person filing an income tax return would pay on that amount. Multiply the result by 10 and that is the tax. It sounds complicated but it really isn't. To illustrate how great the savings are, here is a table that shows the actual result.

If the lump-sum payment is	Normal* tax liability	Tax using 10-year averaging	Savings
$ 5,000	$ 810	$ 350	$ 460
10,000	1,850	700	1,150
25,000	6,020	2,420	3,600
50,000	17,060	8,160	8,900
100,000	42,060	20,900	21,160

*Based on joint return with no other taxable income, after taking deductions and exemptions.

Defined Benefit-Keogh. There is a particularly interesting way the Congress has made Keogh Plans more generous. It is especially worth considering if you start while you are young. Since this is a book on dealing with money problems in retirement, this discussion will just touch the highlights. It is called a *defined benefit* because you may actually structure it to give you the monthly income you will want when you retire at age 65. Using an IRS formula-based table of the percentages of your earnings, which may be applied at different ages, the program is designed to accumulate enough money to buy a straight life annuity contract that will pay you the defined benefit you want. There are limits, of course. The top amount you are allowed to contribute per year on a tax-deferred basis is in the neighborhood of $11,000. The percentages of income permitted on the basis of your age when you start this plan apply to your top annual earnings with a limit of $50,000. You may not pile up more than is actually needed to produce the maximum retirement defined income benefit. If, therefore, thanks to good investment results, your account builds up too much, your annual contributions have to be reduced.

How your money is invested. You make that decision. IRS rules make it essential that the money going into any type of Keogh Plan, and its investments, be in the hands of a custodian. Otherwise there would be no way of policing the fact that you are not entitled to any of it until the times and conditions specified. Beyond that you have broad choices. Banks, thrift institutions, insurance companies and mutual funds have custodial agreements for Keogh and other qualified retirement plans. That, in itself, indicates how flexible your choice of investment may be. The custodians do not say how the money in your Keogh account should be employed. You do. You can, for instance, adopt a mutual fund dedicated to capital growth and at a later period instruct that the account's assets be transferred to another fund that has income as its objective, under the same management.

Individual Retirement Accounts. Nobody is left out in the cold when it comes to tax sheltered retirement plans. If you are not in a business or profession of your own and the organization you work for has no plan, or you are not eligible to take part, you still have a place to go. You may have your own Individual Retirement Account — an IRA.

In many respects an IRA is like a Keogh Plan. The money you contribute to your IRA, and all of its earnings, are free of current taxes — and the contributions are deductible from taxable income. The major difference is that the dollar limit is lower — $2,000. The times and circumstances when you can take your money out are identical.

One individual feature is that a husband and wife may each have an IRA even if only one of them is earning money. The dollar limit on the combined accounts is $2,250. The best way to handle it is for each to have an IRA with up to $1,125 going into each. If husband and wife both work each may put aside as much as $2,000 a year in separate IRA's. Unlike Keogh there are no limits based on percentages of earnings.

The one other important difference is the taxation of the accumulation, if you take it in a lump sum. With the Keogh Plan you saw the advantage of *10-year averaging*. When you withdraw your money from an IRA, you may use *5-year averaging*. The principal is the same. The advantage is less, but so is the amount of money involved. As is true of Keogh, you are in charge when it comes to putting your IRA money where it will be working as you want it to be working. The same rules apply.

The 1981 Reagan tax cuts not only increased IRA contributions to $2,000, but, for the first time, provided that participants in a company sponsored retirement plan could make deductible contributions to their plans of $2,000 a year ($2,250 if there is a non-working spouse). Those contributions can be paid to the plans or, if the terms of the plan don't permit them, employees may establish IRAs to accept the contributions.

Simplified Employees Pension Plan. To take advantage of this one you must be the boss — a business owner. The type of business organization does not matter. Yours can be a corporation, a sole proprietorship, a partnership or a tax exempt non-profit institution. The word *simplified* in the title is totally accurate. When you set up a Keogh Plan as a proprietor you file with IRS and make annual reports. With an SEP you file nothing and no reporting is needed. No trust agreement is involved. All you are supposed to do is to issue to each covered employee a slip of paper IRS supplies, telling them what the basis for the contributions will be. Here, too, you have surprisingly free rein. You decide if you want to make contributions to your account and those of eligible employees based on a fixed amount of money each year, or on a percentage of compensation. If, as time goes by, you decide to make no contributions in certain years, that is entirely up to you. Skipping one or more years does not disturb the tax shelter. Employees are eligible when they are 25 years of age or older and have been working for you for three years or more.

Under this plan the eligible participants, including you, establish IRAs. You may contribute the lesser of $15,000 or 15 percent of income to each — a big jump above normal IRA limits. Although you must contribute the same percentages of compensation for employees as you do for yourself, you may ask for permission from IRS to reduce the contributions you make by whatever Social Security taxes you pay. That can make a dramatic difference in your favor, and in favor of any other highly paid executives.

Look at what can happen. Joe Jojo is president of a small corporation and earns $150,000 a year. Mrs. Jojo is treasurer and is paid $70,000. Two other employees are eligible and must be included. One is Helen, secretary to Joe. Her pay is $24,000. The other is Pete, the office manager, who is paid $18,000. SEP rules do not permit percentages of contributions to apply to anything in excess of $100,000. In order to take advantage of the $15,000 maximum for himself, Joe sets the contributions at the full 15 percent. This becomes the percentage that has to be applied to all.

The corporation's Social Security tax liability is .0665 percent of each employees' pay up to $29,700.

	Salary	Social Security	SEP Contribution	Net contribution after subtracting Social Security
Mr. Jojo	$100,000	$1,975.05	$15,000	$13,024.95
Mrs. Jojo	70,000	1,975.00	10,500	8,525.00
Helen	24,000	1,596.00	3,600	2,004.00
Pete	18,000	997.50	2,700	1,702.50

The owner and his wife do handsomely. All of the contributions are tax deductible. All other IRA rules apply. Employees are allowed to make voluntary contributions to their own accounts sufficient to make up the difference between what goes in and what standard IRA rules permit — $2,000 or $2,250 if there is a non-working spouse.

Rollovers. Of all the tax sheltered retirement methods available, the IRA Rollover may prove to be the most beneficial. You have seen that a regular IRA has a dollar limit of $2,000 and SEP-IRA allows as much as $15,000. Well, the good news is that an IRA Rollover has no dollar or percentage limits. You may put in a half million...a million...any amount.

The heart and soul of the IRA Rollover is that it may be used as your tax sheltered way of receiving lump sum payouts from any qualified plan when it *terminates*. Without the IRA Rollover, as you have seen, when you receive a lump sum payout the tax collector is standing at your side with both hands out. This is the one way to put him off until some future date — the one way of continuing to enjoy the privilege of having that money earn more money free of current taxes.

The word *terminates* is emphasized for a reason. Many people who have heard and read about the IRA Rollover have had the mistaken notion that the only time they can take advantage of it is when they retire. It is much broader.

There are six ways in which a qualified plan may terminate. It doesn't matter if it is a pension plan, a profit-sharing plan or a Keogh you have been involved with as an employee.

1. You retire in the customary time and manner
2. You take early retirement at age 59½ or later
3. Your employing company goes out of business
4. Your company decides to drop the plan
5. Your employer sells the business and the new owner does not continue with the plan
6. You die

When a plan terminates you are paid everything that has accumulated for credit to your account. If you have been in a qualified retirement plan you undoubtedly are familiar with the word *vesting*. To any plan participant, *vesting* is an important word. It relates to the amount of money credited to your name that really is yours. The average plan has rules that say that not one penny of that money truly is yours unless you have been a participant for ten years.

Terminations can change those terms. When a plan is terminated because a company goes out of business, drops the plan or sells out without arrangements for the new owners to maintain the plan, you become fully vested automatically. If you die you become fully vested and your surviving spouse or your estate get the payout. The great likelihood is that by the time you reach retirement age — even for early retirement — you will have become fully vested in the normal manner. Even if the company you work for goes bankrupt you not only become fully vested but there is no need to fear that the accumulation in your name is lost. Any organization that has a qualified retirement plan is required to have all the assets of that plan in the hands of a custodian. That money may not be touched by any creditors.

There is even a seventh situation when the lump sum payout from a plan may be rolled over. If you resign before age 59½ in order to retire or to go into some other work, and you are partially or fully vested, you are allowed to rollover whatever payment you receive.

The IRA Rollover is not a good choice if your total payout is $20,000 or less. It may not be a good choice compared with 10-year averaging. You or an advisor must put the figures on paper before you make the decision.

There are rules to be observed if you decide that the rollover privilege suits you best:

- The IRA Rollover is yours to use if your participation in a plan has been as an employee. You may not use it if you are an employer or a sole owner.
- You may rollover the entire lump sum paid to you minus any voluntary contributions you may have made while the plan was in effect. Whatever your voluntary contributions *earned* may stay in.

- You do not have to roll over the total sum paid out. You may keep any portion out of the rollover but you will pay ordinary income tax on what you keep out. It is not subject to 10-year averaging.
- The rollover must take place within 60 days of the time the payout is received by you. The spouse of a participant who dies is also required to observe the 60-day rule.
- If property other than money — such as securities constitutes the payout you receive, this is what you must rollover. No substitutions may be made.
- You must establish your own Individual Retirement Account (IRA) to receive your rollover. If you already have an IRA it may not be used for this purpose. Under these circumstances you are permitted to have two IRAs.
- At no time may you add anything to your Rollover IRA.
- A Rollover IRA may not be used as collateral for a loan.
- If, after establishing a Rollover IRA you become a participant in another qualified plan, and the rules of that plan permit, you may make another tax-free rollover from your IRA to the new plan. (There is a distinct advantage to this. When the new qualified plan terminates you may use 10-year averaging to reduce your taxes.)
- You may not take money out of your IRA Rollover until age $59\frac{1}{2}$ and you must start taking money out by age $70\frac{1}{2}$. When you withdraw money you will pay income taxes at your regular rate. No 10-year averaging is allowed and no part of the withdrawal may be declared to be a capital gain.

As is true of a standard IRA, you have various choices regarding how the money in the account is to be invested. You may choose any of the permitted options.

You are not bound to whatever funding was used in the terminating plan. If the custodian of the new account will accept nothing but money and you are to be paid in something other than money, be sure to ask the custodian of the terminating plan to *convert the payout to cash before* it is paid to you.

Tax shelters

Until 1976 there were so many types of tax sheltered investments to choose from it would take an entire book to discuss them all. A tax sheltered investment is an investment that permits you to postpone taxes on any income it pays and/or enables you to take tax deductions based on "paper losses." Most of the highly imaginative ones and a major part of the most appealing tax benefits were wiped out by the Tax Reform Act of 1976. And that isn't all bad news. A good many of the so-called tax shelters offered thoroughly bad business propositions because of big tax savings. The tax saving had its attractions for people in the top brackets, provided they were confident the IRS would not successfully challenge the tax benefit.

Tax sheltered investments are not for everyone. Federal and state laws require that the limited partners in most publicly offered tax shelter programs be in the 50 percent tax bracket; that they have assets of at least $100,000 not including home, car and similar possessions. Most tax shelters are high risk ventures. If you meet the Federal and state qualifications, perhaps the tax advantages are all you need and want — how the enterprise fares from a strict profit and loss standpoint is a secondary consideration. If these conditions do not apply to you, it might to wiser to look elsewhere for places to invest. The major element that the Tax Reform Act of 1976 almost eliminated was what was called the *non-recourse loan*. A publishing venture, for example, would be started by some people who would establish themselves as the *general partners*. They would solicit investment from a number of *limited partners*. In addition to the money put into the venture by the limited partners the general partners would go to the bank and borrow. The end result was that the partnership might have $100,000 put in by the limited partners and $500,000 loaned by the bank. The bank loan put no responsibility on the limited partners. They could never be called on to help make good any part of that loan no matter what happened. That is why it is called a *non-recourse loan*. The particularly happy news to the limited partners was that they could share in the tax deductions created by the grand total of the investment, which included the bank loan. It was not unusual for the limited partners to be able to enjoy deductions amounting to four and five times their actual investments. The situation was eye-popping — and you can see why IRS and the Congress took a dim view of the whole procedure.

The '76 Act put an end to non-recourse loans, and the tax savings they created, in everything except real estate limited partnerships. The new rules state that you may not take deductions on anything beyond the *money at risk* — the dollars you actually invest. The big tax advantage of non-recourse loans was permitted to stand for real estate limited partnerships simply because the government saw reason to encourage more investment in building. For the same reason, the '76 Tax Reform Act did not excessively reduce the tax advantages enjoyed by oil and gas exploration investments.

Reasonably attractive and sound tax sheltered investments that offer you a combination of tax savings and growth potential are comparatively limited today. In addition to real estate and oil and gas, the others that may be worth investigation are equipment leasing, cattle breeding and a few others.

When contemplating any tax sheltered investments, there are some important things to keep in mind:

1. Don't be misled about what you will save in taxes. If you see that a tax shelter gives you a hundred percent tax deduction in the first year, this does *not* mean that you can invest $5,000 and take $5,000 off of the taxes you otherwise would have paid. Your actual saving is based on your top bracket. You deduct $5,000 from your taxable income, for example, and if you are in the 50% tax bracket your actual tax saving amounts to $2,500. Furthermore, the tax shelter gives you a tax saving *this* year. Eventually you pay.
2. How firm is the tax advantage? Is it likely to be challenged by IRS and rejected?
3. Putting the tax aspect aside, is it a reasonable business proposition? Would you think about making the investment if there were no tax angle?

Real Estate Limited Partnerships. Securities dealers make these available. You may invest in some with as little as $2,500. The beauty of real estate is that the one investment can give you income, growth opportunities, tax shelter, and leverage (earning income and sharing in profits from a bigger capital investment than you made.) Also, you do not have to possess the experience and knowledge a businesslike real estate investment demands. Chosen with care, your limited partnership investment brings with it the skills of highly capable operators.

The leverage portion is made possible by the non-recourse loan — the money the general partners borrow for which you have no repayment obligations. As noted earlier, this is the only type of investment where you can have a non-recourse loan amplifying your tax savings, income and profits. Because of that advantage, you can have situations where you can deduct from your tax bill every penny you invest, and enjoy tax savings on the income produced, for as long as eight or more years. In many programs you can recapture your total investment within five years, and still own the equity you bought. The equity will continue to produce income and can, eventually, bring you a capital gain when the property is sold.

Until recently, real estate limited partnerships created one problem for people approaching or in retirement — liquidity. Getting out of a real estate limited partnership before it has run its full course — the sale of the property at the end of a relatively long time — is not simple. Limited partners do not generally have an easy time selling their interests. Sometimes the general partners or other limited partners will be interested in buying. Beyond that there are difficulties. There is at least one organization that offers to purchase units owned by limited partners. It is the Liquidity Fund in Emeryville, California. The general partners have to agree to the transfer of ownership — to date Liquidity Fund has encountered little difficulty in that area.

This, for example, is typical language appearing on the front page of a real estate limited partnership prospectus; *"The Units are not freely transferable and no public market for the Units presently exists or is likely to develop. Accordingly, the Units should be purchased only as a long-term investment, since Limited Partners may not be able to liquidate their investments in the event of an emergency or for any other reason."* Liquidity Fund, if it continues to thrive, undoubtedly will attract competitors. The problem of liquidity may become minor.

Oil and Gas Exploration. Even though the 1976 Tax Reform Act took away the attraction of non-recourse loans in oil and gas limited partnerships, this remains one of the most popular tax sheltered investments. It is still quite desirable as a tax favored investment and it does carry the romantic lure of the possibility of hitting a gusher.

An oil and gas limited partnership may be an SEC registered public offering or it may be what is called a private placement. Private placements are generally considerably smaller in terms of total investment, and they are severely restricted as to the number of people who may be offered the opportunity to invest. Despite that, private placements account for about twice as many invested dollars as do the public offerings. Both types are usually sold by investment firms.

There are various types of ventures. It breaks down to three basic ways to go. When you put your money into an oil and gas exploration venture you can be investing in drillings to be done in fields that currently have successfully operating wells. That is the conservative approach. The new drilling is done right in the midst of on-going producers and the likelihood of hitting oil is, of course, very high...almost certain. A venture of this type, understandably, even though it is successful, will not give its investors great profits. The people who own the land where the drilling takes place know what they have and charge an exploratory driller accordingly. The charge may take the form of a considerable percentage of whatever income results, plus a sizeable fee for leasing the ground. As with most things in life, you get what you pay for, and drilling in *producing areas* commands high pay in return for sharply reduced risks.

Next along the line is drilling in *proven areas*. This amounts to doing the exploration in the vicinity of producing wells but not as close as in the first situation.

And then there is *wildcatting*. Wildcatting is to sink the holes in virgin territory on the basis of studies made by geologists. These studies tend to show that there is reason to suspect that the explorations will pay off. They seldom do, but if and when they do, since no premium had to be paid for leasing the ground — and no one was in a position to demand an outlandish percentage of any income — wildcatting can pay off handsomely.

The average oil and gas limited partnership brings together some of each. It might package fifty or more explorations in as many places. Typically, in a fifty drilling venture, ten might be in producing ground, thirty-five in proven areas and five would be wildcatters. There are almost bound to be some winners in the mix, and they will help to compensate for the losers. If one of the wildcatters should become a producer, the whole venture could be most profitable.

Of the money you invest in oil and gas drilling ventures you may deduct 100 percent for the dry holes — the unsuccessful ones. Your deductions for those that produce will be from 60 to 80 percent. On top of that, 22 percent of the income realized from the producing wells is tax free. That is what is known as the *oil depletion allowance*. The allowance will be reduced. By 1984 it will be 15 percent.

The Securities and Exchange Commission warns that there are a number of oil and gas offerings that are fraudulent. They advise that you take great care to check on the authenticity of any you are considering. If it is a public offering you must be given a prospectus. If you have questions about the validity of the things you have been told or have read, do not hesitate to contact the Securities and Exchange Commission's Consumer Affairs Office, 500 North Capitol Street, Washington, D.C. 20001, or one of the SEC's regional or branch offices. The phone number of the Consumer Affairs office in Washington is (202) 523-5516.

Government Oil and Gas Lotteries. You may have received in the mail or have read in a magazine or newspaper advertisements telling how you can be helped to "Strike It Rich" by winning a free oil and gas lease on Federal land. You pay the advertiser a fee and other costs for doing the filing for you and your name will be included in the drawing. You may be one of the many lucky people who get a free lease on ground where oil is found. You'll become wealthy overnight.

The U.S. Department of the Interior warns that this may not be quite as rosy a picture as has been painted. Here are the facts:

There are certain parts of the United States where the government encourages exploratory drilling for oil and gas. These lands fall into two categories: the places the U.S. Geological Survey has designated as known geological formations where producing wells have been developed. These leases are offered to competent people on a competitive basis. Then there is the second category of Federal land outside of the established geological areas. All is not oil that glitters. Leases to explore these lands are offered on a non-competitive basis, by lottery and without charge.

Interior explains the reason for the free lottery method of offering these leases. *"Before 1960, these tracts were offered on a first-come first-served basis. When particularly promising tracts were due to be posted as available, long lines formed at the land offices. Fights often broke out, disrupting business, injuring employees trying to control the crowds. To establish an orderly and fair system of awarding these noncompetitive leases, the simultaneous oil and gas drawings were developed."*

Each State Office of the Bureau of Land Management prepares a monthly list of the lands to be included in the lottery within its jurisdiction. These lists can be obtained by writing for them and paying fees ranging from $2 to $5. You mail in your application and your name goes in the hopper.

The only land where leases are obtainable in this manner are those that formerly were included in competitive oil and gas leases that expired, terminated or were relinquished or cancelled. Your chance of winning a free lease is remote. In 1977, for example, two and a half million people competed for nine thousand leases. And if you win a lease, your parcel may have no potential for oil or gas. The Department of Interior says that most have no value at all.

Chapter Four

More Income Through Securities

To be sure that we are walking down the same street together let's synchronize our language. Because they have no occasion to deal with them on a regular basis, a good many people find a degree of confusion about *income, yield, annualized yield, dividends* and *interest.*

Income is the simplest because it really says what it is: what comes in. If you earn money that comes to you in terms of wages, commissions, royalties or profits from a business you operate — that is *earned income.* But no matter where it comes from or how it is created, whatever assets come in to you is income.

Yield describes income from an investment. There are many types of investments. Some produce interest and some produce dividends. We will get to them in a moment.

Annualized yield is a term normally used when looking ahead. It is used to give a fairly accurate estimate of what your yield will be for 12 months, based on the yield being realized today remaining unchanged. Annualized yield makes it easier to picture what an investment will provide for you — and to make intelligent comparisons with other investments.

Dividends are earned by investments in common stocks. When you invest in a corporation's common stock you really become a part-owner of that business. If the corporation makes profits, its board of directors decide what part of those profits should be kept as a means of helping the business to carry out plans that require financing; to pay for research, development, exploration or expansion; to reduce long-term debts; to hold as a reserve; and what part to pay out to you and the company's other shareholders as dividends — your share of the profits that are not retained to make your company stronger. They may decide to pay no dividends at times even when profits are good. On the other hand, it is not unusual for a company that regularly does pay dividends to its shareholders to do so even at times when it has losses. They do that for any of several reasons, such as their knowledge that the loss was due to highly unusual circumstances and not to business being bad, and that the next period will produce more than enough profit to make up for the dividend payment for the past and present periods. Or they may feel that not paying dividends might create a lack of confidence in the company resulting in a drop in the price people are willing to pay for the company stock. Were that to happen, the value of your stock would suffer. Normally, companies try to pay pretty much the same dividend each year with an "extra" at year end when profits are rising.

Interest is paid when you lend money. You lend money to banks and thrift institutions when you make deposits to savings and checking accounts, initiate or renew certificates of deposit, etc. You lend money to corporations when you invest in their bonds. You lend money to the government when you invest in EE and HH Bonds, Treasury Bills, municipal bonds, etc. These are called *debt securities*. The interest you are paid amounts to rent for the use of your money.

There are those who feel more secure investing in debts — bank and thrift accounts, corporate bonds and government securities. The amount of interest is usually guaranteed and you are further assured that, at the end of a specified time period, you will be repaid the exact amount you put in. Common stock investments are quite different. There are no guarantees. You literally go in business with the corporations whose stocks you buy. In many respects buying yourself part-ownership in a company through investments in common stocks is the same as going into business for yourself. You may make a good living, you may hit it big, you may lose some money or you may go broke.

One big difference between investing in stock and owning a business, however, is that you can unload a stock that begins to turn down. You can do it instantly. Walking away from a business of your own can be agonizingly slow, and far more costly.

On the surface it may appear that investing in debt securities is a losing game in an inflationary economy. In addition to interest, you get back no more and no less than you put in. That need not be the case. You do get back exactly what you invest *if you wait for the security to mature* — by holding a ten year bond for the full ten years. But were you to buy a ten year bond paying 15 percent interest and three years later newly introduced bonds are paying only 9 percent interest, you would have no problem selling your 15 percent bond at a good profit. We will take a closer look at bonds, preferred stock, convertible securities and some other kinds of investments a little later.

Common stocks

Right now we are interested in common stocks and how they might help you to keep your financial head above the waves of inflation and taxation.

There are well over 30,000 stocks available for investment. Many of them are *listed* on various stock exchanges, such as the New York Stock Exchange, the American Stock Exchange, the Pacific Coast Stock Exchange, and so on. Others are bought and sold in what is called the *over-the-counter market*. Being listed on an exchange does not mean that a company's stock is better or worse than those on the over-the-counter market. Generally it simply means that the companies whose shares are listed are big; that a great quantity of their shares are traded pretty regularly that it is necessary to have them bought and sold in one place where it is easy and quick to match up buy and sell orders. That is the major reason for the existence of the different exchanges.

Investment dealers, securities dealers, stock brokerage firms — just different terms for one kind of business — are the organizations you go to when you want to buy or sell securities. As a matter of fact, these companies sell more than securities. Most of them deal in life insurance, real estate investments, financial planning services and a variety of tax shelters. All of which is good. Gone are the days when they sold just stocks and bonds. Gone are the days when insurance agents sold only insurance. Most of them offer mutual funds, and some have other financial products and services. The less brokers and agents are confined to one type of product, the less bias is present when you go to them for guidance. The investment firms maintain lines of information that permit them to learn who has the over-the-counter issues available for sale, at what price — who is interested in buying them and at what price. They frequently have valuable information on a variety of securities, in particular on those that are head-quartered in their own regions.

There may be certain advantages in dealing with a branch of a national New York Stock Exchange organization, for they support fine research departments and offer a broad variety of services. On the other hand, the ultimate thing individual investors need is a man or woman who will take a sincere interest in them and their needs, someone with knowledge, integrity, empathy and energy. Such an ideal person to handle your investments needs is just as liable to be found in a single office, modest size company as in the offices of the biggest of the big.

You are protected. Just about all broker-dealer firms in the United States or its territories, offering the public their services in the buying and selling of various types of securities, are automatically members of the Securities Investor Protection Corporation (SIPC). In many ways this resembles FDIC and FSLIC, the organizations that insure your bank and savings and loan accounts for as much as $100,000. SIPC goes further. If a broker-dealer you have been doing business with should fail, SIPC sees to it that any securities registered in your name, or about to be registered in your name, are returned to you. As to cash and any other assets, you will receive your pro-rated share of all that remains and SIPC will reimburse you for the difference. Their reimbursement has certain top limits. They will reimburse you for as much as $100,000 of cash or up to $500,000 for securities, but no more than a total of $500,000 taking both into account. There is no reimbursement for commodity contracts or commodity options, or for unregistered investment contracts.

If you have more than one account with a broker-dealer — one in your name and one in your spouse's name and a joint account — each of them enjoys the full coverage. You can have accounts in several different firms and you are fully protected in each.

SIPC's resources come from assessments on the firms covered. At this writing their statement shows a balance in excess of $200 million. In the event of certain emergency situations, SIPC may borrow up to $1 billion from the U.S. Treasury. Five of the seven members of SIPC's Board of Directors are appointed by the President of the United States.

Keeping track. Stocks listed on the major exchanges are reported in big city newspapers, the Wall Street Journal and other financial papers every day. A number of the other exchanges have their stocks reported in the papers as well. Once a week some of the more active over-the-counter stocks are shown.

This is how the reports of daily changes appear:

1	2	3	4	5	6	7	8	9	10	11
52 Weeks				**Yld**	**P-E**	**Sales**				**Net**
High	**Low**	**Stocks**	**Div.**	**%**	**Ratio**	**100s**	**High**	**Low**	**Close**	**Chg.**
62⅜	48¾	UniNV	4.94e	8.7	4	2	56¾	56¾	56¾ +	⅜
63¼	45⅝	UCamp	2.80	5.8	7	186	48¼	47¾	47⅞ +	⅛
62⅛	44⅞	UnCarb	3.40	7.2	5	1258	47⅛	46⅜	47 +	⅛
12¼	7⅛	UnComr	.20	1.8	8	79	10⅞	10⅝	10⅞ −	¼
9¼	4⅛	UnionC	.29t	5.8	6	39	5⅛	4⅞	5 −	⅛
12	9⅞	UnElec	1.52	15.	6	650	10⅜	10⅛	10¼ +	⅛
27	20½	UnEl	pf3.50	15.	..	z600	23	22½	23 +1	
34¾	25½	UnEl	pf4.50	16.	..	z100	28	28	28 −	½
47	39¾	UnEl	pf 6.40	17.	..	z2500	38⅛	d38⅛	38⅛ −1⅝	
62	46⅜	UEI	pfL 8	16.	..	z180	50½	49	49 −	½
15⅞	12¾	UnEl	pf2.13	16.	..	7	13½	13⅛	13⅛ −	⅞
22⅜	18	UnEl	pf2.72	15.	..	2	18	18	18	
54	45	UnEl	pf 7.44	17.	..	2	45	d44	45	
59¾	47½	UEI	pfH 8	16.	..	12	49	48½	48½ +	½
56½	28¼	UOilCal	1	2.6	10	3136	38⅜	36⅝	38¼ +2	
96¼	42½	UnPac	1.60	3.2	12	1405	49⅞	48½	49⅞ +1½	
10⅜	4⅜	Uniroyl		..	5	361	8½	8¼	8½ +	⅛
44¾	25½	Uniryl	pf	..	..	z180	39¼	39¼	39¼ +	¼

The columns are numbered for this illustration to clarify what each one means:

1. This is the highest price the stock has sold for during the past 52 weeks.
2. This is the lowest price for the same period of time.
3. The name of the stock, abbreviated. If you buy a stock find out what its symbol is or you may have trouble finding it.
4. The dividend in dollars and cents. The figure shown is the amount of dividend paid annually for each share, based on what was paid the last quarter or the last semi-annual payment.
5. The annualized yield — the percentage of income you can anticipate for the full year if the dividend holds firm. It is based on the stock's value that particular day.
6. This figure is called the PE ratio... the Price-Earnings ratio. Today's price is divided by the company's earnings. For example: if a stock's present value is $20 a share and it is earning $2 a share per year, the Price-Earnings ratio is 10. This is regarded as an important yardstick in deciding if a stock is underpriced or over-priced. It takes a lot of know-how to make that determination. If a company is booming, growing at an unusually rapid pace, its popularity as an exciting growth opportunity can boost that PE ratio to a very high figure, which may or may not be justified. On the other hand, there are stocks with very low PE's that hardly ever rise in value.
7. Another indication of a stock of interest is the degree of buying and selling going on. This figure shows the number of shares traded on the previous day.
8. The top figure paid the day before.
9. The bottom figure paid on the day before.

10. The final price of the day.

11. How much the price changed yesterday compared with the previous business day, shown in dollars.

Growth of capital is vital. Inflation and the urgent need to fight it with all the knowledge and energy at your command has been discussed in earlier pages. It will be discussed throughout the book. Few aspects of your financial life can approach it in importance. You have seen how *total return* is one of the better techniques that may be used.

Common stock investments offer the broadest highway to opportunities to put the *total return* idea to work and to putting your money where it has a chance of growing as fast or faster than living costs.

For the person planning ahead, with retirement five, ten or more years ahead, growth of capital has exceptional attractions. Dividends and interest are taxed in the years they are paid. It doesn't matter if you take them in cash or have them reinvested. Growth in value is another and better story. No matter how much your investment may grow, none of the extra dollars accumulating for you are taxed until you sell. When those profits are taxed you pay a lower tax than you pay for dividends and interest. For example: if you bought a stock at least one year ago, sell it now and have $1,000 profit, your tax, no matter what your tax bracket happens to be, will be no more than $200 (20 percent). IRS grants you an 80 percent exemption from tax liability on long-term (over one year) capital gains. Speaking of taxes, $200 of dividend or interest income is tax free each year. A couple enjoys a $400 tax exemption. The free ride on taxation of profits until you sell is a real bonus. In effect, the taxes are postponed. You have the money that otherwise would have been paid to IRS still at work and capable of earning more money for you. Of course the profits that remain untaxed because you have not sold could disappear, if the value of your investment goes down. It is to be hoped that your profits will continue to increase.

If you are retired and are depending on *total return* to increase your ability to stay ahead of rising living costs, growth remains a key element in the picture. It is unlikely that dividend income, after taxes, will be able to win the race by itself. You need the combination of growth and income.

Where do you look for growth? For most people, when asked where to look for growth of invested capital, the first things that come to mind are real estate, gold, other precious metals, diamonds, rare coins, art objects and other collectibles. That is natural since so much has been written and said about the great growth in each of these fields. In a later chapter they will be discussed in some detail. At this moment those investments have had dramatic growth. That is history. That was yesterday. There can be and probably will be more growth, but the point is, these are by no means underpriced investment opportunities. If you are looking for growth now, it seems logical to look for it where you aren't too late — where you can hope to participate in *growth to come.*

There is nothing I know about, despite impressive increases in value, where prices are the same or less than they were 15 years ago, except stocks — the common stocks of America's corporations. Take a long and thoughtful look at these facts:

- The Dow Jones Industrial Average is the most popular measurement of the price the public is paying for the stocks listed on the New York Stock Exchange.

- In 1966 the Dow Jones Industrial Average was:
  1000

- Since 1966 the *dividends* being paid by those stocks have increased:

  300%

- Since 1966 the *book value* of those stocks has increased: 100%
  (Book value is the present true value of all of a corporation's hard assets: buildings, real estate, machinery, money in the bank, money due, inventory, supplies, etc.)

- In 1981 the Dow Jones Industrial Average was:
  **1000

Imagine that: Dividends tripled... tangible liquidation value doubled... but the prices being paid for the shares of those stocks is right where it was 15 years ago.

It is the last bargain of its kind available.

The question that leaps to mind is, why is this true? There are many theories. My conviction is that throughout that 15 year period we have gone through an era of enormous uncertainty. Where there is uncertainty there is fear. When there is fear, people are inclined to extremes. In financial matters, one extreme is the desperate acceptance of speculative risk; the other is ultra conservatism. In desperate efforts to keep pace, there were those who turned to gold, silver, real estate, diamonds and collectibles such as rare coins, art, antiques. The impetus they supplied fanned the inflationary fires and values soared upward. The

---

**In 1966 and in 1981 the Dow Jones Industrial Average was slightly over or slightly under 1000 and at no time in the intervening years did it go more than a few points beyond 1000.

resulting publicity made the flames leap still higher. Fear of loss drove the conservatives to banks, savings and loan institutions and credit unions.

The motivating force in both directions was fear-inspired emotion. The risk takers were winners. The conservatives were not. The common stocks, removed from the extremes, just stood still despite their expanding health and strength. Ever rising prices and the increasing rate of taxation, frustrating those getting cost of living increases, added to financial confusion. Over periods extending for more than 15 years, securities values have inevitably grown to reflect their worth and to catch up with and exceed living costs. The 15 years of stagnation, resisting the strong upward trends of profits, dividends, basic values and living costs, have made stocks like a coiled spring waiting to be released.

Trading on the widespread concern and confusion, the pied pipers of panic found their own financial salvation by selling books and subscription services warning that the *great collapse* was about to descend on us; that currency, government and industry were doomed. The panic prophets advocated getting rid of everything you owned, buying gold, canned food, a rifle, and finding a cave in the hills.

What they failed to explain was who would buy the gold and with what when money became worthless and what you would live on without income while waiting for the universal disaster.

And then in 1981 the most prominent of these very successful disaster sellers started saying that stocks and bonds appeared to be good buys and perhaps it was not the best time to buy gold.

The one acceptable thought advanced by the doom-sayers was that it is not wise to put your faith in dollars.

Dollars once were promissory notes guaranteeing that they were exchangeable for their face value in gold or in silver. No longer is that true. They are simply printed pieces of paper that we exchange for goods and services. How much they can be exchanged for constantly changes. That is why you cannot rely on dollars. Ownership puts solidity under your financial structure. Ownership capable of producing income you can use for the day-to-day exchanges for food, shelter and all your other needs and niceties becomes particularly desirable if that income has the chance to increase as prices increase and if the basic investment in ownership has the chance to grow more valuable.

Common stocks represent ownership. They give you five splendid benefits:

1. They can give you income capable of increasing.
2. They have value capable of growing.
3. They can be sold at any time without difficulty.
4. You have extensive choices.
5. *They are the only bargains left.*

The question of risk has kept a good many people away from common stock investments. There are multitudes who say, "I want the comfort of knowing that my dollars are guaranteed and that I have regular, unchanging income I can rely on."

In the intensive care wards of modern hospitals, people with heart conditions are wired to screens over their beds. The screens, like television sets, show each patient's heart at work. The visibility of the screens enables nurses, interns and doctors working and passing through the ward to be constantly watchful.

When the line on a screen is pulsating, up and down, that is *life:*

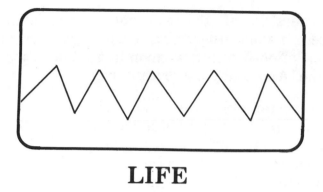

LIFE

When the line is steady...unmoving...that is *death.*

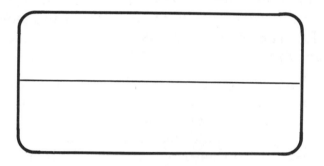

DEATH

In an inflationary economy the same is true of your capital. With the cost of living constantly in motion, relentlessly moving higher as it has done since 1954, having your money where it is nailed down to a fixed rate of return is *death of spending power.* There is no comfort there. It is the awesome price paid for dollar guarantees. It is a positive, known risk of loss. It is not a conservative use of money. It is a reckless refusal to face financial facts.

Ownership of the common stocks of soundly financed, historically strong, progressive corporations is an inflation-fighting weapon available to just about everyone. And today *the price is right.*

Unquestionably, there are some new unproven companies in emerging industries whose stocks will be the spectacular superstars in the months and years ahead. Investors owning those stocks will make a great deal of money. But the effort to find them and the immense good luck of putting your money in the right ones involves very high risks — risks to be taken only by those who can accept the losses without damaging their life styles. Getting into a bright and promising new industry seems alluring. It pays to remember, though, that once automobiles fit that description and more than 2500 U.S. companies have been in that field. Today there are four.

How do you go about it? With more than 30,000 stocks to choose from how do you make wise and appropriate selections? The older you are the more you should be careful to avoid major losses, since you don't have the time to recapture them, as younger people do. How do you pick the potential winners without taking dangerous chances of losing too much? How do you find the right kind of expert who will give you the time and attention you want? How can you be interesting enough as a stock broker's customer to feel that you are getting the attention you crave? How do you measure the honesty and sincerity of the person or people you entrust your assets to? Maybe you are fortunate. You may know a stock broker so long and so well that you can put your faith in his or her hands with total confidence. The chances are that most of the brokers you are liable to meet will be dedicated, capable people. They are employed because investigation has shown them to fit that description. They have seen and have learned that the more they put your interests above all else, the more they will be rewarded by your loyalty and your willingness to bring other clients to them.

But there is this to consider. The first time I ever invested, I went to a good friend. I knew him and I knew the fine reputation he had earned. When I told him that I wanted to open an account and have him in charge, he proved his honesty at once. He said, "I'm delighted and flattered that you want me to be your broker and I'll do everything I can to get you off to a sound start. Once you are invested, however, don't count on my watching your account day after day and calling you each time a change should be considered. I have too many clients. It is impossible for me to conscientiously study and evaluate their investments on a daily basis. If you feel the need for change, you come to me."

It was disappointing, but it made sense. His experience, ability and character attracted many people which made him too busy to give any of them full-time attention. *If he had less to recommend him, he would have had more time for me.*

Investing for yourself

Can you do it yourself? Perhaps. Quite a few people have. They have steeped themselves in the intricacies of investing; they follow the market hour after hour and day after day; and in time, after many errors and understanding what those errors were, they have become good at handling their own investments. It certainly can be done. But while many, in terms of numbers, have succeeded in reaching that degree of knowledge, skill and emotional control — and the item of control may be the most vital — percentage-wise very few reach that level of competence.

If you want to try, there are six key considerations:

1. *Give yourself sources of dependable information.* That is a fundamental need. There are services you can subscribe to that bring to your attention industries and corporations they have studied in depth and that they believe to be excellent candidates for investment. Value Line, Standard & Poor's, Moody's are a few of the better known sources. They will show you what they have learned and why they favor some issues, why they are changing their thinking about others, and why they feel that certain ones should be sold or avoided. Other services concentrate on general market studies, and their findings can serve as a basis for investment decisions on timing... is this a time to buy, to sell, to just mark time?

Publications such as the Wall Street Journal, Forbes, Barrons and others are filled with facts that are important to investors. Trade publications are must reading for those who have special interest in certain industries.

Many of the brokerage houses make their research studies available. Priceless information can be obtained from such reports.

2. *What industries appeal to you?* If what you read, hear and think leads you to believe that certain industries are going to increase in importance and profits in the months and years ahead, narrow your studies to them. Choose those which, after analysis, seem to be the best contenders. And then take the next step — find out which companies look like the best operators within those industries. Which have the longest record for good dividends and growth? Which have the strongest financial structures? Which are most heavily involved in innovation and may be on the verge of a breakthrough that can greatly increase their volume of

sales and their profits? And look for the opposite — the ones to avoid.

3. *What will your investment earn for you?* That's a crucial question if your retirement income is giving you problems. There are plenty of stocks of companies with good growth potential that also have good current yields. If the stocks you are weighing do not pay at least as much as a passbook account, perhaps you should keep searching.

4. *Have you looked at their financial statements?* Reading financial statements is no easy task. One thing that is not too hard to isolate, however, is the relationship of current assets to current liabilities — what the company has and what it owes. If the assets are not twice as big as the current debts, be wary. Long-term debt is another matter. Long-term debt is borrowings, such as those debts represented by bond issues. Here, too, if the long-term debt looks too big in relation to the company's worth, tread with care.

5. *Spread yourself.* No matter how promising the investment in one company may appear to be, there always are unknown possibilities. A well accepted rule of cautious investing is to put your assets in a number of places. If one or two turn sour, you can be salvaged by the good results of the others. Rule of thumb: invest in not less than five issues in no less than three industries.

6. *Curb your emotions.* If you have carefully researched your investment and have found that experienced experts are moving in the same direction, never let temporary good or bad news impel you to panic. As has been demonstrated so often, a news item such as the illness of the President can drive the market down to a remarkable extent. That has absolutely no bearing on your investment unless you had planned to move in and out of some issues within a matter of days. The chances are that you are in for a relatively long-term. Don't run for cover because of a short-term event and short-term reaction to the event. The market is an instant barometer of emotions but, given enough time, it reflects values. At times when news unrelated to the companies you are involved with causes the value of your stocks to fall, that is the time to give long and hard thought to buying more — not selling. It is bargain time. And, of course, the opposite can serve you too. If good national or international news sends values soaring, that could be the right time to sell enough of your investments to recapture what you paid, letting the remainder stay in there waiting for the future, solid increases in value that you anticipated — increases that are likely to endure.

Don't torment yourself over, "If only I had bought when..." or "If only I had sold..." Years ago a man I knew told me the story of a missed opportunity that took place when he was very young. He had a savings account in a bank near the store where he was clerking. One day he went to the bank manager. He said, "I just learned about a new company that is in an interesting business and they have stock selling for twenty-five cents a share. I want to draw $250 and buy 1000 shares."

"What kind of a company is it?" the banker asked.

"It's something called Radio Corporation of America."

"Save your money," the banker said. "I'm not going to let you throw it away on a wild speculation like that."

Telling me of this, my friend Henry said, "You know, I have figured that if I had invested that $250, the value of my investment today would be about $8 million. But," he went on, "I don't feel badly about it. I know that when those shares had doubled in price, gone to 50¢, I would have sold."

Emotions play such a vital role. You have to know yourself. With an abundance of knowledge and guidance, you can still be a miserable investor if your emotions are likely to override good judgment. It is one reason why so many intelligent, careful investors will not do it themselves. They turn to financial planners. They put their investments in the hands of investment advisors, give brokers discretionary accounts or invest in mutual funds. Let's sort these out.

Financial planners. They are relatively new on the scene and come in a number of shapes and sizes. There are one person operations and everything in between those and the financial planning divisions of some of the largest national New York Stock Exchange firms. Most financial planners will probe deeply into a client's assets, liabilities, family status, sources of income, age, health, desires and more. They will produce a finely detailed plan. The plan will cover what percentage of the client's income and assets should be invested in each of various ways; will cover tax problems, trusts, wills, estate matters, possible gift programs, insurance of all types and more. Some planners will be in a position to sell some of the investments suggested and will earn commissions from those sales. Others will confine themselves to planning. Those who can offer investments and insurance may make no charge for the planning, content with the potential commissions. Some will reduce fees by whatever commissions are realized. Some will charge fees and commissions. Some, who do none of the investing for their clients, work on fees only. Fees differ considerably, frequently based on the client's net worth.

The manner in which fees and commissions are charged should not be the chief basis for selecting a financial planner. The soundest course is to go to a planner whom people have recommended. If you have no recommenders, never hesitate to ask any financial planner exactly how he operates, what your costs will be and, above all, who are some of the clients you could phone or visit. Planners will ask you endless questions. Do not hesitate to ask a few of your own.

The financial planning divisions of brokerage firms put some people on guard because they fear that they may be pressured into buying whatever the firm wishes to sell. Probably not. The people who staff the financial planning divisions seldom participate in any commissions the firm may earn resulting from financial planning suggestions. A sizeable organization is apt to have in their employ an assortment of individuals with expertise in the many areas that financial planning covers. That can be very much to your advantage.

Look for financial planners in your yellow pages. Best of all, look for them by asking enough people you know until you have found one or more who have had good results.

Investment advisors. Investment advisors generally have no connection with the sale of any financial products. They are what the title indicates — advisors. The advice they sell, on a fee basis, stems from their continuous, in-depth study of security markets, the general economy, legislation that could have impact on securities as a whole or on the securities of specific industries, even on specific companies. Today, many advisors make use of computer technology, using them to keep comprehensive records of those stocks and bonds that are particularly interesting to them, and to store all of the facts about their clients' investments.

More often than not, investment advisors ask for and are given the complete right to make buying and selling decisions for their individual clients without prior consultation. Some clients, however, require that each purchase or sale be discussed with them and will ask for some restrictions on the advisor's freedom to act. The relationship between the advisor and his client starts with an initial interview, establishing what assets are to be turned over to the advisor, what securities the client currently owns, what the client wants in terms of income, growth, high or low risk, speculation, conservation, and so on.

Investment advisors usually will not accept accounts unless they have some established minimums of capital to place in their hands. $50,000 to $100,000 is at the lower end of the scale.

Discretionary Accounts. The normal way to work with an investment dealer is to have your broker buy and sell securities for you on the basis of your own ideas, those the two of you have discussed, or suggestions originating with the broker. Some, but not all, broker-dealer firms will suggest discretionary accounts to some people. It is a desirable way of handling the investments of those who travel a great deal, who are ill, or who shun the emotional problems of making such decisions.

Mutual Funds

For those who don't want to, or feel ill equipped to move into the securities market place on their own — for those who do not have sufficient capital to go to an investment advisor, to attract a good broker or financial planner — nothing compares with mutual funds.

A really good broker, as you have seen, is handicapped by having too many clients. In no way, even by putting all clients and their investments into a computer, can the busy broker keep the needs and interest of each one on the top of his mind as the daily changes in the market place occur. It is impossible. In contrast, a mutual fund's investments are managed by a team of experienced professionals of proven ability. That is how they got their jobs. That is how they keep their jobs. This team serves *one client* — the fund. If you are an investor in the shares of that fund it is because the fund's goals and basic policies match your goals and basic policies. As a matter of realistic fact, therefore, you have that team of full time professionals devoting their entire time and attention to you.

If you are not thoroughly familiar with mutual funds, it will pay to take a moment to acquaint yourself with what they are and how they work.

History buffs may disagree, but the general concensus is that the underlying idea goes back to the days when merchant owners of sailing ships would send their ships off to sea loaded with precious cargo. They had to wait anxiously for months before they knew if the ship had come back to port with hoped for profits, or had been lost at sea. A merchant's entire fortune could be lost if the ship was destroyed by storm or taken by pirates. This might have been the historic beginning of ulcers as well as mutual funds. In time, the thought was advanced that a group of merchants would do well to pool their ships and cargos, each owning a share in keeping with his contribution to the pool. If, under those circumstances, 15 or 20 ships left home and a few never returned, the losses would be more than compensated for by the profits of those that made the round trip in safety.

That is a mutual fund. Thousands of investors buy shares of a mutual fund. The professional investment managers of the fund employ that large pool of capital, investing it in many different securities they have thoroughly investigated — securities they have reason to believe will enable the fund to reach its announced goals. If a few prove disappointing, the happier results of the others can more than counterbalance them. The managers continue to study, watch, analyze. They visit with corporations they have invested in, and others they are considering. As they see the need to do so, they sell some of their investments and add others. As more investors send money to the fund by buying shares, or by having their dividends reinvested for them, the managers add to the fund's investments.

Stop at this point. Picture the things made possible for you, things that you probably could not do on your own.

1. You have the team of full-time professionals working for you to select the best places they can find for your dollars to be working.
2. That team is active every business day watching over your dollars, poised to move with knowledge and speed whenever they see opportunity for change and improvement.
3. No matter how small an amount of money you turned over to them, they have spread that money over scores of securities, eliminating the threat of your *single ship sinking.*

And that is just a start. There are no time limitations on how long your money must be invested. The funds themselves buy back your shares on request. Whether you will get back more, less or the same number of dollars you put in depends on a number of things, not least of which is your decision as to when to redeem your shares. You are in control and can move your money in and out as you please.

Mutual funds can be divided into three sections:

Section 1. *The traditional types of mutual funds.* These funds have as their goals:

- *Growth of capital.* Growth fund managers try to make profits for you by investing in stocks they expect to grow in value.

- *Growth plus income.* Instead of concentrating entirely on profits, the managers choose some stocks that pay generous dividends. They do not, necessarily, buy stocks that offer both growth and income but will buy some of each.
- *Some growth, some income and some investments, such as bonds and preferred stocks, that tend to protect your invested dollars.* The mixture creates a balance that is quite conservative.
- *High income.* Full attention is given to income and the use of techniques that may help to make the income greater than usual.
- *Good income.* The managers specialize in securities paying better income than most but select those taking less risk that the *high income* funds involve.

How well has Section 1 been doing? On January 1, 1981, here is what the 5 year period looked like:

Cost of living increased 56.3%

Average listed common stock, based on Standard & Poor's 500, increased 91.4%

Average mutual funds (listed above) increased 140.0%

Two things to recognize when looking at those figures: the increase shown for the mutual funds and Standard & Poor's reflect only the *price per share*. They do not include dividends. In other words, *total return* was better. The second point is that the 140% increase in value of the mutual funds is the *average*. Average represents the best of the poor and the poorest of the best. With a little study when selecting a mutual fund, you could have done considerably better.

Section 2. *The money market funds.* These are structured just like the funds in Section 1 but the investments made by the managers are quite different. No common stocks are bought. No effort is made to create profits. The money market funds exist for highest possible income and for the lowest possible risk.

They are called money market funds because the investment are in what people on Wall Street and the banks call *money market instruments*. Until money market funds came along the only buyers of money market instruments were the biggest, wealthiest financial institutions — banks, insurance companies and such. The reason for this exclusivity is that the financial items that produce the highest interest also command the highest minimum purchase price... $100,000, $250,000 on up.

Money market instruments include obligations of the United States Government, those of the biggest and strongest banks and the biggest and strongest corporations — obligations, remember, not common stock.

Another aspect of money market funds that makes them different is that they won't buy any securities that do not involve a promise to pay back every penny invested within a *short period of time* — every penny invested plus a high rate of interest until repayment is made. The short time involved can be as brief as a few days but is never more than a year. The short term is important. The shorter the life of any interest paying debt instrument, the less the price of that security will fluctuate. That follows because the issuer is going to pay full price for it in the near future. That is one of the major reasons why there is so little risk in money market funds. The price the fund pays for the securities it buys is not likely to increase or decrease, to any material extent, between the time it is bought and the time it is redeemed.

The interesting result of that absence of price movement is that the money market funds went to the Securities and Exchange Commission and asked for a special ruling. The prices paid when investing, and the prices people get on redemption for all other types of mutual funds, vary from day to day. The prices, referred to as the *net asset value*, are based on the true value of all the securities the fund holds at the close of the market each business day. The total value of all of a mutual fund's securities are added, divided by the number of all of shares the public owns, and that is the net asset value. If the general stock market had a strong *up* day, the net asset value will reflect it, being higher than the day before. The opposite will usually be true on a day when the market values of securities dropped. The money market funds said to the SEC, "There is going to be so little change in the net asset value of our shares that we would like to give our investors the peace of mind and the convenience of paying a uniform price when they buy and getting the same price when they sell."

The permission was given. The little bit of change that takes place is added to or subtracted from the daily income the money market funds earn. The price per share for many of the money market funds is an unchanging $1.00.

With that kind of pricing it became easy for the money market funds to win the cooperation of their banks when they asked them to give their shareholders the privilege of writing checks against their money market fund investments. Checks in the amount of $500 or more are written by the shareholders. Not only is that a fine accommodation, it is also a source of extra profit for the investor: John Johnson, for example, owes $2500 to IRS for taxes. He writes a money market check for that amount and mails it to Washington. Until IRS gets the check, records it, deposits it and its bank gets the check to the fund's bank for clearance, John Johnson's

$2500 keeps on earning a handsome rate of daily interest. Earning income on money you have already spent is definitely desirable.

Some worry about the ruling that the smallest check you may write is for $500. It can be an advantage: Mrs. Hudson needs $84 to pay a bill. She writes a check, payable to herself... a check on her money market fund for $500. She deposits the check in her regular bank checking account, pays the $84 bill out of that account and writes a $400 check to her money market fund, mailing it the same day. The chances are good that the $400 will be back to work before the $500 check she deposited in her bank checking account clears the fund's bank. Until it clears she will be earning daily interest on that $500.

Some of the money market funds restrict their investments to debt instruments of the United States government, its territories, agencies and instrumentalities. No type of investment is safer. These are backed by the full financial strength and the taxing power of the U.S. Risk is eliminated as much as it is possible to eliminate risk. If the U.S. failed to meet its obligations on these securities, then just about everything in the country would become worthless. Because of the exceptional safety of the money market funds, investing exclusively in government issues yields about one percent less than the other money market funds.

At the time this book was written, the general money market funds were yielding approximately 17% interest.

Section 3. *Tax-free municipal bond mutual funds and unit trusts.* Before describing the tax-free municipal bond mutual funds and unit investment trusts, a few lines about municipal bonds themselves.

The reason we have tax-free municipal bonds is that the writers of our Constitution, in their determination to protect the rights of the states, wove into our laws the fact that the federal government may not tax securities issued by the states and the states may not tax federal issues. When a city, for example, needs money to build a bridge, it sells municipal bonds. The interest paid to those who buy the bonds are free of federal tax. Generally they are also free of state taxes for the residents of that state, though other states may impose income taxes on the interest. On the other hand, the interest paid by federal securities, while subject to federal tax, are tax-free in the states.

You may invest directly in municipal bond issues. There are some problems. Municipal issues have long lives. Just as is true of the bonds sold by corporations, they have a specific number of years to run before they mature — before the issuer redeems the bonds for the price paid when the bonds were originally issued. Municipal bonds normally have 20 to 30 year maturities. Every village, town, city, state, territory and possession of the United States may use municipal bonds to finance their roads, bridges, water works, schools and considerably more. Take the number of issues that come to market and add to that the fact that throughout their long lives they are traded — bought and sold; it is not too surprising to find that there are about 150,000 municipal bond issues to choose from.

Customarily, municipal issues are sold in $5000 units. If you want the risk reduction of having your investment spread over a number of the tax-free issues, it takes a good deal of money.

The problem of selection involves checking out the quality, safety and the comparative yields offered, plus the amount of money required. You can see that hand-picking some individual issues may not be the best path to take. There is also another aspect to weigh with great care which is related to the long lives of the issues. The City of Somewhere's Sewer Bonds paying 10 percent interest might look very good to you. If your top tax bracket is 50 percent you would have to find something in a taxable security that pays 20 percent to give you the same net yield. But in a few years your 10 percent return might not look quite as good if, at that time, new municipal bonds are paying 12 or 14 percent. Were you to have reason to sell your 10 percent bonds you would be forced to sell them at a discount or nobody would have reason to buy them from you. The opposite could be true, but the point to appreciate is that there is a risk involved if you fail to hold your bonds until they mature. Even if you do hold them until the end of the line your investment is earning less for you than the higher yielding new issues produce. That, too, can be looked upon as a loss.

Tax-free municipal bond mutual funds. There are about 50 of them. They have all the characteristics of the traditional mutual funds in Section 1. The managers use the investors' money to buy scores of tax-free issues they have studied and like. They constantly are on the alert for reasons to sell some and to buy others. Shareholders may buy and sell their shares whenever they please. Since the managers do adjust the funds' holdings this is one way of having investment in tax-free issues with a varying yield. If yields rise the funds are going to be well aware of what is taking place. The managers will sell off some lower yielding issues and will invest in the providers of greater income. If yields are moving downhill, the chances are that there will be very little buying and selling. The funds will be content with what they have and, presumably, so will the investors.

Tax-free municipal bond unit trusts. In some ways a unit trust is like a mutual fund and in some vital ways it is quite different. It does have investments in a number of different municipal bond issues, making it possible for people to share in the ownership of them all without having the immense sums of money that would be needed otherwise. To that extent the unit trusts and the traditional mutual funds are alike. The great differences are: there is no active management and there is no variation in the yield. This can give you a fine advantage. If, for example, a tax-free trust has a very high yield and from all you can learn the specialists expect yields to start coming down, your investment in the trust locks-in that favorable yield for you. It will remain at the same level for many years. Not only does that assure you of good tax-free income, it creates the possibility of your being able to sell your units at a fine profit when yields do fall.

The sponsors of a tax-free unit investment trust will invest several millions of dollars of its own money in a variety of carefully chosen municipal bond issues. It then will divide the entire package up into units — $250, $500, $1,000 or, perhaps, $5,000 per unit — and offer them to the public. As an investor, you know what the yield will be when you invest, and that is what you will receive over the years. As the bonds the trust holds mature, the unit holders share the proceeds. In time all of the issues will have matured and everything will have been paid out to the investors and that is the end.

Not many unit holders wait that long. For any number of reasons they or their estates may want out earlier. There is a market for their units. It is called a *secondary* market. When selling in the secondary market a unit holder may make a profit or take a loss, depending on how current yields compare with the yield their units earn.

All of the units are sold within a relatively short period of time, sometimes as quickly as a week or two. After that the sponsors have no further units for sale of that particular trust. There is no way, therefore, to permit you to reinvest your tax-free distributions in the trust. Some unit trust sponsors, however, also have tax-free mutual funds and make it easy for unit trust investors to have their distributions automatically invested in the fund shares, permitting them to compound tax-free income.

In addition to long-term tax-free unit trusts there are unit trusts invested in *medium-term* issues and some with *short-term* issues. The medium-term trusts will have bonds maturing in about ten years. Short-term trust investments mature in five or six years. The medium-term and short-term trusts can be used to fill some special needs. Here's an example:

John Sire is 55 years old. His earnings are good. His taxes are high. He knows that company policy will force him to retire in five years. At that time his income will be lower and he'll want to add to it. John has some stocks earning a generous yield and he is paying his top tax on that yield. He sells the stock and puts the proceeds into a medium-term tax-free unit investment trust. The result will be that the trust income coming to him until retirement will be free of tax. He will also arrange to have it automatically invested in the unit trust sponsor's tax-free municipal bond fund. When John retires he will instruct the trust to send him the interest payments but the previous payments that went into the fund will not be disturbed. They will continue to earn tax-free income which will be reinvested in the fund's shares. At the time when John retires the bonds in his medium-term trust will start maturing and he will share in the pay-outs resulting from the redemptions, adding to the spending money he will be getting for a period of time. When that runs out, he can turn to the accumulation that has been compounding tax-free in the fund.

Load and No-Load funds. The terms *load* and *no-load* are heard frequently. Nothing complicated. A *load* mutual fund is one that requires you to pay a sales commission when you invest. A *no-load* fund may be bought free of any sales charge. Neither exact any charge when you redeem your shares.

Because there is a sales commission linked to the *load* funds, they are offered by investment dealers and by those life insurance agents who are licensed to sell mutual funds as well as insurance. There are better than 500 mutual funds and many people are happy to have the help of a knowledgeable person in selecting the right fund and having guidance as to the wisest way to make the investment. Others are content to do it themselves by writing to the *no-load funds* or phoning them to request copies of their prospectuses and application forms.

There is no real difference between the performances of the load and no-load funds. Logically, there is no reason why there should be, since the professional investment management of any fund is not linked to the selling process.

Most money market funds are *no-load*. About one third of the tax-free funds are no-load. The traditional mutual funds (Section 1) are mostly *load funds* but a growing number are *no-load*.

(The Investment Company Institute, at 1775 K Street, N.W., Washington, D.C. 20006, will send you a free list of the various funds, showing the nature of each. Over 560 funds are members of the Institute.)

(The No-Load Mutual Fund Association, Valley Forge, PA 19481, will send you a directory of their members. There is a $1.00 charge.)

The question is, do you want the guidance of a trained person? Are you willing to pay the cost? *Usually about 8 or 8½ percent* of your original investment for the traditional funds and about half of that for the tax-free unit trust? The answer can be related to the various service features you may draw upon. In your original choice of which fund to invest in, and how to use the service to your best advantage, are the areas where guidance may be of great value.

Mutual fund services. There are many of them, but there are a few that have particular interest for you if you are approaching retirement or have retired.

Distributions. There are two types of distributions made by the mutual funds in Section 1: dividends and net profits realized from the sale of securities out of the fund's investments. You have some choices. You may take both in cash. You may take dividends in cash and have the profits reinvested, at no charge, buying extra shares for your account. You may say that you want both reinvested, at no charge in most cases. Your decision, of course, will depend on your cash needs. And you are free to change your instructions whenever you want.

Exchange privilege. If you invest in a mutual fund that is one of a family of funds managed by one organization, you have the right to have your investment moved from one fund to another when and if you see good reason to do so. If, for instance, you owned shares in the group's fund concentrating on *high income* and you came to the conclusion that securities values were moving up at a strong, prolonged rate, you might conclude that your needs might be better served in their growth fund. It is only necessary to write a letter to the fund requesting that they transfer your assets from the income fund to the growth fund. You will immediately have an equal dollar worth of shares of the growth fund and be out of the income fund at no expense. Exchanges may be made as frequently as you choose.

Withdrawal plans. Mutual fund withdrawal plans permit you to have monthly checks in whatever amount you decide you want. What you ask for must be based on sound judgment, of course, or you can hurt yourself.

Here is an illustration of a well considered use of the withdrawal plan service:

Sam and Sally Sawyer have been accumulating money in a growth mutual fund for a number of years. The combination of the money they put in, growth in value and the compounding power they enjoyed by having all dividends and profits reinvested, have brought the value of the account to $60,000. When Sam retired, the Sawyers sold the home they had lived in for several decades. They realized a substantial profit and, thanks to their ages, $125,000 of it was tax-free. They used a large part of the proceeds from the home sale to buy a modest dwelling in a retirement village. The balance, $32,000, was added to their mutual fund account, giving them $92,000 altogether.

Monthly maintenance payments on their retirement home came to $250 and real estate taxes amounted to another $100 each month. Sam and Sally met with the broker who handled their fund investments and after listening to his advice, they decided to have the fund put the $92,000 into a withdrawal plan account. In doing so they instructed the fund to send them monthly checks based on a withdrawal equal to 8 percent a year. They added to those instructions that at the end of each calendar year the fund was to recalculate what the monthly checks would amount to, holding to the 8 percent but applied to the value of their shares at that time. The broker pointed out what this would mean:

1. In the first year the checks would amount to $613 a month. The fund would send a check for $350 to the retirement village maintenance office for the maintenance fees and taxes. The Sawyers would get another check for the balance, adding to their dollars for living.
2. Over the years the fund had done well meeting its growth goals, and they had reason to hope and

believe that the value of their investment would continue to grow. If that proved to be the case, then their 8 percent a year withdrawals, based on whatever the value of their shares amounted to at the end of each year, probably would give them the equal of yearly cost of living increases.

3. Total return for this fund had averaged 15 percent a year over a period of time. The withdrawal of 8 percent would permit the value of the account to grow and that would mean that they did not have to fear that they might outlive the source of those monthly checks.

4. Realistically, they had to appreciate the fact that there could be some years when the value of their shares would go down. If they held firmly to their 8 percent withdrawal instructions, the monthly checks would be reduced in the years when share value declined. If the economy moved into a true depression, they could expect that the value of the shares would reflect that situation, as would the cash flowing to them.

5. The decision they would make as to how to take their withdrawals is not a contract. They would be free to change instructions at any time. During a year when values were depressed, they could tell the fund to increase the percentage of the withdrawals. In good years, if they did not need increased income, they could build their reserve by issuing instructions to decrease the withdrawal percentage.

6. There might come times when they wanted an extra sum of money to handle an unexpected expense, to pay for a trip abroad...for any reason. They have full control of their money in the account and can, therefore, write to the fund requesting an extra check for whatever they need.

7. Although the monthly checks make a

withdrawal plan seem like an annuity, it is not. There are two critical differences: (1) There is no guaranteed lifetime payout; (2) Whatever was left in the account when both Sam and Sally are gone would go to their heirs, not to the fund.

8. The funds generally charge nothing for withdrawal plan services.

The way the fund provides the monthly checks, and any other withdrawals, is by redeeming a sufficient number of shares to handle the sum needed. They even deal in fractions of shares — enabling them to fill your requests to the penny. When you have a withdrawal plan you must have all dividend and profit distributions reinvested. You can see that were you to go overboard in the payouts you ask for you can, in time, use up all of your shares. That would be the end of the plan and the account.

Withdrawal plans are great if used properly. You can use them to handle long-term payments of uniform sums to others. You can, if you have good reason to do so, deliberately plan on using the entire investment by taking big monthly sums over a predetermined period of time. People use them to pay rent, mortgages, alimony, child support, insurance premiums...anything you want.

Before leaving the world of securities there are some other sources of income that should be mentioned.

Preferred stocks. Common stocks do not have unchanging yields. Dividends will rise and fall because profits are either good or bad, or because they company's directors decide to use profits for expansion, for acquisitions, for paying off long-term debts, for greater research and development, or because they are pessimistic about the year ahead. As you saw in the description of common stocks at the beginning of this chapter, they may increase dividends because they have ended a period of expansion and so on. Regardless of the reasons, dividends paid by common stocks will vary. Preferred stocks have fixed rates of dividends, and some are very attractive. A corporation's bonds usually pay a little more, but the reasons preferred stocks are called *preferred* is that the holders stand at the front of the line if the company gets into financial trouble. Whatever assets there are go first to the preferred stockholders.

Convertible bonds. An investment in a convertible issue gives you steady, unchanging income — it also gives you a chance to make profits if the common stock of the same company has a significant increase in value. When you have a convertible bond your purchase provides you with a guarantee that you have the right to exchange your convertible for a certain number of shares of the common stock at a specified price per share. Unless you pay a big premium for your convertible when you first make the investment, the common stock price is going to be quite a big lower than the price at which you may exercise the exchange privilege. If you have a strong conviction that the common stock will have a substantial rise in value it could be a good approach. There are a few factors that make convertible bonds interesting. One is that the fixed rate of interest paid by the bond frequently is higher than the dividend paid by the common stock. Second, should the stock go down in value, instead of going up, the probability is that the bond's value will not fall as much.

Here is a typical example of investing in a preferred issue successfully: You buy the convertible bonds of the Master Mustard Corp. It has a 7 percent yield. At the time when you buy Mustard, its common stock is $15 a share. Your convertible guarantees that you may convert to the common when the market value is $28 a share, and it details how many common stock shares you will have for each convertible bond share you exchange. At some time in the future the shares of Master Mustard common stock reach $28 and keep climbing. You are not required to convert at any point, so when you are satisfied that you are going to see the common go well beyond the conversion rate, you make the exchange. You may decide to sell the common, or if it looks as though the value will keep going up, you may decide to hold the common stock for future sale. In either event you have a profit.

Options. There are a number of ways of dealing in options. Some are highly speculative and some are fairly conservative. The conservative way of playing the option game is a means of increasing your income from stocks you own.

You own, for example, 200 shares of Green Apples Corp. You paid $50 a share and that is about what it is today. Just as there are exchanges, such as the New York Stock Exchange, for dealing with trades of common stocks, there are option exchanges. If Green Apples is listed on one or more of the option exchanges you may sell an option on your stock.

Selling an option amounts to this: Speculator Steve pays you a price which gives him the right — the option — to buy your 200 shares for $50 a share at any time during the next 6 months. He pays about $6 a share for the option: $1200. The $1200, less commission to the broker who handles the transaction, goes to you. Steve isn't going to buy your stock unless and until he can do so at a profit. Since he has spent $1200 he wouldn't have anything to gain until the stock went beyond $56 a share — $6 a share over the $50 he would pay you. That would only give him enough to recapture his $1200. If he has no reason to buy your stock at the end of the six month period that is the end. He is out $1200 and you are ahead $1200. Suppose the stock went to $60 a share during that period. He would exercise his right and buy you out. If you had never sold the option you could have sold your stock at $60 for a $2000 profit. But you did sell the option. You have not experienced a loss however. You collected $50 a share for your Green Apples from Steve. This is what you paid and you have the $1200 option fee. It is not a bad way to go.

The example above describes what is called a *covered option*. That term simply means that you sold the option on stock you actually owned. You may, if you want, sell an option on stocks you do not own. That adds some substantial risk. In the Green Apples example, had you sold the option without owning the stock, and Steve called on you to deliver the 200 shares when the value was $60 per share, you would have been required to buy the stock at $60 a share and sell it to him at $50 a share. Your loss of $2000 would be eased by the $1200 you had collected, but you would be out $800. If the option had run its six month course without Steve having reason to ask you to deliver, you would have the $1200 in pocket without having invested anything. But suppose Green Apples went to $70 a share?

The people who buy options put the entire option price at risk. If they have no reason to exercise their right to buy, they lose everything they spent to buy the option. People buy options when they think the stock is likely to have a strong increase in value. Steve, for instance, could have bought 200 shares of Green Apples at $50. But he chose to put $1200 at risk instead of tying up $10,000. Perhaps he knew that his $10,000 put to work someplace else could earn more than the $1200 cost of the option during the six month option period.

There are other things that can be done with options that are complex and can be interesting. Sophisticated uses of options call for sophisticated people calling the moves. If the subject appeals to you find a broker who has earned an excellent reputation for smart option trading.

EE U.S. Government Savings Bonds. The yield at this writing is 9 percent. You pay no state tax on the yield, ever. Federal tax is deferred until the bonds mature or when you redeem them before maturity. When you buy them you pay only half of the face value. At maturity you are paid the full face value, which is the manner in which the interest is paid. They are available in denominations ranging from $50 to $10,000. You may not redeem EE bonds for six months after purchase. They take a full eight years to reach maturity. If, after the first 6 months, you decide to redeem your bonds, the interest that would have been paid at the end of the 8 year term is reduced in keeping with the number of years short of maturity. When your bonds mature at the expiration of 8 years they no longer earn anything. When redeemed at that point, the Federal taxes that had been deferred become payable, unless you exchange your double E bonds for double H bonds.

HH U.S. Government Savings Bonds. These you buy for full face value in denominations ranging from $500 to $10,000. The yield at present is 8½ percent paid to you by check at 6-month intervals. As is true of EE bonds, the interest is tax-free in so far as the states are concerned, and Federal taxes are deferred until redemption. Maturity is in 10 years. There is no penalty if you redeem before maturity. If you exchange EE bonds for HH bonds, prolonging the Federal tax deferral, here too there is no penalty if you redeem before maturity.

Do you have any of the old E or H bonds? Any that were issued between May, 1941 and April, 1952, had 40 years to mature. Between 1981 and 1992, depending on the date of the original issue, they will stop having any yield. There is no point in keeping them. When you cash them in, the deferred Federal taxes will be payable unless you exchange them for today's HH bonds. In that case the deferral remains in force and you will be collecting the semi-annual 8½ percent yield.

Chapter Five

How a
Retired Person
Should Invest

GAIL WINSLOW, *Vice-Chairman of Ferris & Co., members of the New York Stock Exchange, is one of the best known and most highly respected women brokers in the United States. She is in demand as a speaker and a writer. Her many brokerage clients venerate her. I sat at Gail's desk with a tape recorder and asked her what advice she would give to people in or approaching retirement.*

As people retire they should simplify their lives and look at things entirely differently because the investments that were correct for them in the period when they were working may well not be correct — not appropriate, for the years of retirement. I think that one thing that they might do is to sit down and review their situation with their advisor, perhaps a different advisor. Perhaps they should talk with whoever has been their advisor and then go and get some other ideas from some other person or people. The person that has been advising them has been looking at things from a very different set of circumstances and may find it difficult to make the transition. I don't mean that they should drop everybody. They might say to their old advisor, "Pretend that I am an entirely different client. And pretend that what I have now is not necessarily what I have, but let's say I just had cash. What would you have me invest in, knowing my new set of circumstances?" See if your advisor, your broker, your whomever it is in the case of investments, can make that transition with you. If no ideas are forthcoming perhaps you had best look for a new advisor, someone who may specialize in investments for a retired person. In addition to that, I feel very strongly that retired people think of whether they want to set up trusts, whether they want to have powers of attorney given to people, as far as their securities are concerned. Perhaps they want to retire their portfolio of securities and choose as their advisor a mutual fund or an investment counselor; a person to whom they pay a fee to advise and watch over their portfolio of securities. This, of course, is appropriate for a person who has rather a considerable sum of money. Usually we think of the investment counselor as being appropriate for someone who has in excess of $100,000 worth of investments in stocks and bonds. For the person with amounts under that, a good mutual fund or a certain mutual fund might be particularly good for them.

Stop keeping securities in your safe deposit box. I find so many people keep their stocks in the safe deposit box because they have some idea that stockbrokers are not trustworthy and that if the stock brokerage house went out of business or something that they would lose money. There is an insurance program now to which almost all brokers are a member. All companies that are member firms of the New York Stock Exchange must be. A person's securities are protected against any kind of loss by an insurance program up to a very, very large amount of money. So I feel it's perfectly safe to leave your securities with your broker. When you leave your securities with your broker you can leave them either in what we call safe keeping in your name or in the name of the brokerage house. If they're in safe keeping in your name, then it means that the certificates themselves are merely being held by the broker in his vault. Your name remains on the certificate, the corporation still has you as a stockholder of record, the dividends are still sent to you directly by the corporation as are the annual reports, quarterly reports, and proxies. However, that still means that you as a retired person who may be planning to travel has to worry about your dividends coming in and how they get from your house into your bank account. It also means that if the company pays a stock dividend or a stock split, those new certificates are going to be sent by the company directly to you. To me the better way of keeping your securities is in what we call *street name*, or the name of the brokerage house. In that case your name is removed from the roles of stockholders with the corporation.

Let's say you own AT&T and the name that goes on the books, instead of your own, is that of your brokerage house — the XYZ stockbrokerage firm. You say, "Gee is that safe?" Oh yes it is! First of all, you have receipts. Secondly, you have statements that come to you every time there is any activity in the account, either dividends deposited or stocks bought or sold. And what happens is that, in addition to your name going off the books and the name of the brokerage house going on, dividends are going to be sent directly to the brokerage house. They will credit them to your account. Not only are the cash dividends and interest earned on your bonds handled that way, but in addition, stock dividends and/or stock splits are sent directly to the brokerage firm and credited to your account. It keeps your account in a good workable form. Your dividends all come in there, your stocks all come in there, and you receive a record every single month. Most brokerage firms — a vast majority of them — do not charge for this service. Then you can tell your broker what you want done with your dividends. Brokerage firms obviously can't send out dividend checks every day. What most of them do is to send them out at the end of the month. You could say to your broker, "I'd like the check to come at home," or you could say to your broker, "Would you please, every month, send my check for deposit directly to checking account #_____ at such-and-such a bank?" They will send it directly to your bank for you.

When a client of mine has a very large investment which he or she has had over the years, which four times a year will pay a particularly large dividend, they may say to me. "I know that a dividend is coming in on the first of the month. Will you please send it out to me immediately?" And, of course, it will be done. If you want your broker to automatically do something, he generally will do it once a month. If you want a dividend that comes in in-between, just call your broker and it can be sent out to you directly or sent to your bank directly in between dividend sendout time. At the end of the year, when you have a *street name* account your tax reporting is much easier. You can just report dividends paid by XYZ brokerage house: $243.66. You don't have to break it down with AT&T — $5.80, Exxon - $1.00 and General Motors — $2.00. You just lump them together under who the paying person was and that is how your brokerage firm will report to the government. There is no need to break down as long as all the dividends were collected by the brokerage house. So it makes it a lot easier for you.

Now that you've retired and perhaps have more free time, this is an excellent time to bring your own records at home up to date. If you have securities that you inherited or changed their names or anything like that, document them and record the original cost as well as where you actually did get XYZ stock, so that if you die or become incapacitated, your house is in order.

Married people lead such busy lives these days that they don't have a chance to sit down and go over things together. Now that you're retired, I think it is a great time to share the knowledge and the burden of responsibility of caring for your capital, which is so important now. After all, once you're retired you don't want to have to go back and try to earn that money again. I always say to my clients that the day they retire when they get up in the morning and look in the mirror, they should say to themselves, "I am no longer a speculator, I cannot gamble, I must be an *A-No. 1 investor."* And they have to constantly realize that some of those investments that they made previously may still be excellent investments for someone who is looking for above-average capital appreciation, but that as a retired person they can no longer afford the luxury of speculation.

As a retired investor you must realize that conservation of principal is a very important consideration. In addition to conservation of principal, there is also the necessity, in most cases, of giving yourself high current income, because most of us do not have unlimited amounts of capital but have to have our capital working very hard to produce as much income as possible to supplement retired pay. We must always look for an investment which can appreciate in its income. I'm not talking about a security that you buy at 10 that goes to 20 in its price. But a stock that goes from a $1.00 dividend, to a $1.20 dividend, to a $1.50 dividend, to a $1.75 dividend as the cost of living increases. So when I am working with my clients and looking for securities that will fill these requirements, I have a list of five things that I look at. First of all, I tend to buy large companies. The reason for buying large companies is that they got big somehow because they were doing something right. As very large companies they also are more often than not diversified into many different facets of a particular industry. If they lose out on one part of their industry, or one part of the company is not doing particularly well, oftentimes another part of the company will have a smoother outpouring of earnings over a period of time. Additionally, a large company is often able to compete because of its size, because of its resources, and because, geographically, it is usually spread into many different market places. So I do think that size is important. This is not always the case, and by size I'm usually talking about size within an industry. It may be that the company I'm talking about is minute in comparison to a General Motors or a Standard Oil, or Exxon, but within its industry it is dominant. And so dominance within the industry and size are important to me.

A second consideration is that I find a company that is conservatively capitalized. The capitalization of a corporation means just how the money with which it runs its business is divided. I want to know how much of its capital is from its debt securities, bonds, or preferred stocks which have not a specific time limit to be paid back, but a specific dividend which is supposed to be paid; and how much of their capitalization is made up by common stock. This is very important for the conservative investor. You must remember that the bond holder has to get his interest, and the preferred stockholder has to get his dividend before the common stockholder gets anything. So if there is a great deal of debt and a great deal of preferred stock out, then, if earnings should drop, there might not be anything left for the common stockholder. So the higher percentage of common stock and the smaller the percentage of debt, the happier I am as far as the investment is concerned. I want to make very, very sure in the case of a company that does have debt outstanding and preferred stock, I want to make sure that I can look back at the very worst years; war, famine, recession, or even that horrible old bugaboo word of the 30's, — the depression — and I can see that this is a company that has safely gotten over the shoals of business and international problems — that it has always been able to pay its interest and preferred stock dividends and still had money left for the common stockholder.

The third thing that I look for, for a conservative investor, is the kinds of industries. There are certain industries which fluctuate wildly in good or bad times— the automobile industries, the housing industry, what we call white goods, which aren't white anymore — those nice avocado and golden wheat-colored refrigerators and stoves — these are things that people buy sometimes and sometimes they don't. But there are certain things that the public never seems to be able to do without — food, milk, shoes, gasoline, (although we've certainly been able to cut back on that) the telephone, our banks, our utilities, our medicines, aspirin, Alka Seltzer. These are securities with products or services that the buying public usually continues to buy in good times and in bad. Because of this, their earnings do not fluctuate wildly and therefore their dividends don't fluctuate wildly.

The fourth thing that I look at is the famous one, "Buy low and sell high." I guess it was Bernard Baruch who taught us that regardless of how speculative the stock was, if you could buy it cheaply enough you might have a good speculation. But, on the other hand, the best investment can become a speculation if you pay too much for it. I look back over the years and see some of the places where conservative investors have been hurt — hurt when they have paid too much for a good company. Even AT&T, which, heaven knows, is one of the stand-bys for everybody in the investment field for conservative investors. While AT&T has done what it was supposed to do by continuing to earn more and more money every year and raising its dividends almost every year, the stockmarket during the 60's pushed AT&T up in price to a very unreasonable point. That wasn't AT&T's fault. That was the stockmarket's fault. And people were paying $75.00 or so a share for AT&T almost 20 years ago, and here today, in 1981, AT&T is selling for $50.00 or so a share. That looks like a 30% or so decrease in its price. Well, when you consider the cost of living and what has happened to the dollar — the $75.00 that a person paid for stock back 20 years was worth a lot more than $75.00 is today. It wasn't a matter of what AT&T did. Back in the 60's someone said to me, misunderstanding, "Why does AT&T charge so much for their stock?" It wasn't AT&T; that was the market — the public.

You can go back and see that Sears Roebuck and Eastman Kodak and some of the best stocks out there were bid up to prices that made them no longer sound investments. And so the old adage of buying low and selling high is still important. Usually retired investors are not in and out of the market; they certainly are not and should not be traders. But that does not mean that there are not times when stocks should be sold, and funds put into other investments. There may be times when people should be lowering their holdings of stocks and shifting some of their money into treasury bills, money market funds, savings accounts at commercial banks, or savings and loans.

The fifth thing I look for is a stock that has a long dividend-paying record that over the years has increased. If you find a stock that has paid the same dividend every single year, well, yes, that looks like it's pretty good unless you think that inflation is not going to go away. In effect, if the company has never raised its dividends, it is *lowering* its dividend every year in terms of what you can buy with it. But, I like a company that has paid a dividend all the way thorough the last, oh, 25,

30 years, and, preferably, goes all the way back to World War II. If the company was able to get through World War II and some of the many recessions that we have had since then, that's probably a pretty good test that it is a company of great safety. You really have to go back that far. You should go back and see what it did in good times and bad.

I always like to use an example of my dear mother-in-law who is a very marvelous woman. My mother-in-law was widowed some 22 years ago. And while she was certainly not a trained investment person in any way, and she had not actually handled the investments of the family, she just has done a marvelous job since she became a widow. Yes, I have given her some advice and care but she has good common sense and has studied and read. So it can be done by everyone, regardless of their training. My mother-in-law purchased securities 22 years ago and many of them she purchased from her own good common sense after consulting with me. She bought such stocks as AT&T and General Motors and Chase Manhattan Bank and Hershey Foods and Virginia Electric Power Company and Cheesebrough Ponds — absolutely the types of stocks that, if I could have chosen a portfolio, I would have chosen myself. She's made some changes over the years, but every January or so she would call me and say: "You know, Gail, I did very well last year." Well, during the 50's and 1960 and 1961 this was indeed the case. In 1963 my mother-in-law called me in January and she said, "Gail, I did very well last year." And I said, "Oh no you didn't. The stock-market crashed last year and while it has recovered rather well we had a bad Monday and Tuesday in May and your stocks are still way down from last year." She said, "Oh well, I don't care about whether they are up or down." I said, "You don't?" She said, "No, I'm not going to sell them. I've bought those stocks because I want the income. What I look at each year is what were my dividends last year over the year before, and what were my dividends in relation to how much it cost me to feed myself and clothe myself." And I thought to myself, "My heavens, this woman is a true investor, she has bought her securities as long term investments for what their return will be because, as she said, she doesn't want to sell them anyway."

And that is, in effect, what she's interested in — a good steady dividend and one that has been going up.

Every once in a while over the last 22 years my mother-in-law has called and said, "Such-and-such a company has not continued to raise its dividends. What do you think? Are they going to resume raising their dividends? Are they not making as much as they were? Should we perhaps find something else?" That's the kind of attitude a retired person should take. My mother-in-law is now 83 years old and just as canny as she every was about her investment portfolio. She really is absolutely spectacular.

I think oftentimes we go so hard to try to find a stock that will just pay a high dividend that we don't realize that what we should be looking for is our total return; not just the dividend itself, but the combination of dividend and appreciation of the stock. I'm thinking right now of several stocks that pay 6, 7, 8 percent, not your 10, 11, 12, 13 precent utilities. I think that the companies that have 6, 7, 8, percent perhaps will have *appreciation potential* of 10, 12, 15 percent-a-year. I'm now talking about increases in the market value of the stock, not increasing dividends. You know there is nothing that says you can't sell a few shares of your stock. There is an advantage. While most retired people are in a slightly lower tax bracket the fact remains that you still are probably in *some* kind of a tax bracket. The income that you get from skimming a little off the top by selling a few shares after they have appreciated you report as a long-term capital gain, so, from the tax implication, you are very much better off than if you collect only dividends.

There are very, very few people who have the capabilities of managing their own portfolio. And I certainly feel that the retired person — my golly, unless he or she wants to make a great big hobby of it and spend a great deal of time on it — I think retired people should retire their portfolio of securities and give the proceeds over to someone else to manage. I think mutual funds are an excellent method of investing, giving you someone else, who's a professional, the problem of worrying about it. Or, as I said, with the larger investor the investment counselor or the investment advisor. These are some people who are retired who do know something about it and want to become involved and want to work closely with the broker. For the rest of the people, the person who sells his house, moves into a small apartment and has X number of dollars from the house that he wants to invest, I think he's very much better off sitting down with an investment advisor, or stock broker, who will devise a program for him, and unless he has a very great interest in becoming personally involved, I certainly recommend mutual funds.

When you buy a mutual fund you have three charges. Charges, I always like to explain, like those you'd expect to pay if you were going to join a country club. You'd have an initiation fee; that's the same as the load, or the commission. You pay that only once. When you leave the club you don't get it back and when you leave a mutual fund you don't get it back. But it is a one-time fee, and, by the way, if you are going to be buying into a fund that is part of a family of funds, once you've paid your initiation fee — your load — you have the privilege of switching from one fund to the other within that family of funds without paying an additional load. Second is a management fee. This management fee is like your monthly dues at your country club. You're going to pay those regardless of what happens, just for them to oversee your fund, check on your portfolio, and manage it. This is the money that pays for the salaries of the people who actually manage the investments of the funds and for the people who run the administrative side. That's what they get out of it. That's a very small percentage, a fraction of a percent. The third fee that you have is the commission that is paid by the mutual fund to the broker from whom they buy stocks for the portfolio or through whom they sell stocks from the portfolio. You may have heard about discounts in commissions. The average individual does not get a discount when dealing with a broker who is also his advisor. I know I never give discounts when I'm dealing with clients I'm advising and for whom I'm watching over things in their interests. Very, very, very large clients, including mutual funds who do their own research and make their minds up about what they want to buy and sell for the mutual fund portfolio, use the brokerage house strictly to carry out the orders that they have. And so they actually dictate what they will pay. Here, at our firm, we receive orders from time to time from mutual funds to buy and sell, usually in extremely large sizes; 40,000 shares, 20,000 shares, 10,000 shares, 100,000 shares. They tell us, "We will pay you x number of pennies a share." And so the commissions that are paid by the mutual funds are a fraction of what the individual would pay. It's entirely possible that a 100 shares of stock the individual buys might require a commission of $85 or $90. It is entirely possible that the mutual fund would pay as little as 90 cents for each 100 shares it buys — they may pay as little as 5 cents a share because of the gigantic quantities that they are dealing in and the fact that they are doing all of their own work. So, overall, mutual funds are one of the most reasonable investments you can make, as far as cost of acquistion and the

144   How a Retired Person Should Invest

cost of serving as your professional advisor, because once you join the club your management fee is oftentimes less than the price of a year's subscription to the Wall Street Journal. By the way, they don't send you bills for management fees and the fund's expenses. They take them out of the dividends that they pay you. This could be the smaller investor's most economical way of investing. In addition to that, the sales commission becomes smaller as a percentage of the investment as the investment itself becomes larger. The maximum load that is charged is usually somewhere around 8 percent — the one-time fee on smaller investments. When you get to a point of having invested $10,000 it's smaller — $25,000 still smaller. So, with each investment that is made that goes beyond these particular *breakpoints*, with the next dollar that's invested the commission is lower. The commission is money well spent. It's sort of like saying, "Do you really want to take your own appendix out?" You don't have to go to a doctor and pay him all that fee if you want to do it yourself. Well, you could do it yourself with your money too, but it's not something that I would recommend. The broker is going to earn his money, not just when you invest, but by giving you guidance and help over the years.

Chapter Six

More Income Through Real Estate

What to do about your own home

If you own your home and are in need of more income you have a number of options. According to government statistics the chances are that you *are* a home owner. Their figures show that 72 percent of people over the age of 64 own their own homes. The figure rises to 80 percent when you isolate couples in retirement — and 84 percent of them have paid-off mortgages.

Home values have increased to an astonishing degree over recent years. The awesome growth of a person's equity in his or her home creates an ironic situation. You may be the owner of a fully paid home that has tripled in value but are experiencing financial problems because your utility bills, maintenance and taxes are so heavy. The increase in the value of your home and the increase in the costs of living in it both spring from the same source — inflation. The irony is compounded by the fact that although you have a most impressively valuable property, it appears that there is no way that you can draw upon that value to ease financial pressures. But there are some possibilities.

More than financial questions are involved. Home ownership embraces a great deal of sentiment, which is not something to ignore. A very wise financial decision may not be the best decision if it brings with it unhappiness and enduring regrets. It is fortunate, therefore, that you have a few alternatives to consider.

Refinancing. When mortgage rates are well above 10 percent refinancing is not an easy answer. The only sound reason for refinancing is to give yourself some additional income. If the interest you must pay on a new first or second mortgage is as much or more than what you can earn by investing the refinancing proceeds, there is no point in refinancing. True, mortgage interest is deductible from taxes but that is counterbalanced by the fact that most dividend and interest income is taxable. If mortgage rates drop to 10 percent or less, then some types of refinancing can be very interesting.

Reverse mortgages. A relatively new concept, the reverse mortgage is a possibility. In a nutshell, here is how the reverse mortgage can operate to the advantage of a couple living in a home that is free and clear. Mr. and Mrs. Major's home has a market value of $100,000. They are in the midseventies, retired, and they want additional income. They apply to a savings and loan institution for refinancing assistance. The thrift institution's loan officer says, "Your most advantageous way of refinancing is to use a *reverse mortgage.* We will lend you as much as 80 percent of your home's current value ... $80,000. Here is how this will be handled. We will use the $80,000 to buy an annuity for you. The annuity payments at your age, Mr. Major, will amount to about $12,000 a year. From that will be subtracted the interest payments to us. The remainder will come to you in monthly checks. This will continue as long as either of you lives. When both of you are gone your home will be sold. Out of the proceeds the loan to us will be paid off and the balance will go to your estate."

The annuity purchase is not a requirement but it is a very sound element of this arrangement. Handled in almost any other way there would be the possibility of your living well beyond the life expectancy tables, running out of capital and losing your home. An annutiy guarantees lifelong payments no matter how long you or your spouse may live. It is priceless protection against the possibility of finding yourself homeless at a very old age.

The Federal Home Loan Bank Board approved reverse mortgages in December, 1978. They are very flexible and a variety of arrangements can be made so that they are adjustable to individual situations. At the time that this book is being written, they have no appeal to anyone. Mortgage interest rates are so high that they would absorb the entire annuity payments. If and when the rates fall reverse mortgages can be worth checking out.

Sale leasebacks. This is another novel strategy that permits you to make use of the value of your home without having to give up your right to live in it. An investor buys your home at a discount that can be anything from 15 percent to 30 percent under the fair value at that time. The investor gives you a cash down payment of 10 percent of the purchase price. You and the investor arrive at a mutual agreement as to a reasonable rent you will pay, but he will pay all taxes, insurance and maintenance costs. The buyer makes regular monthly payments to you over a period of 10 or 15 years. He must also purchase a lifetime annuity in your name. That contract will start providing monthly payments for you when he has completed his payments for the home. You are thoroughly protected — you have the original down payment, his continuing payouts followed by the lifelong annuity payments — and you can continue to live in your home for as long as you please at rent that is acceptable to you. The investor enjoys worthwhile benefits, too. He bought your home at a good discount. He has steady rental income and the great possibility of a fine capital gain after you have passed away or have decided to move.

Refinancing your present mortgage. If you have had a mortgage for a number of years and you still owe a balance think twice — perhaps three times — before accepting an offer from your mortgage lender to refinance. It may seem attractive if you are cash shy but it may prove to be extremely expensive. Suppose you have had the mortgage for 10 years and have another 10 years of payments ahead of you. Your original mortgage may have been at a rate in the area of 7 percent. Your lender is paying a lot more than that for money and he makes an offer that looks good to you while it relieves him of continuing to carry your 7 percent loan. Your home has increased in value quite a bit and your friendly banker tells you that you can have a $60,000, 30-year loan at 12 percent, which at the time is 4 percent under the prevailing mortgage loan rate. It looks attractive. You'll have the cash to invest, you are getting a very favorable rate and the loan payments are spread over 30 years.

Before acting stop, look and listen. Listen, in particular, to a good accountant or lawyer. Once your professional advisor has put all of the figures on paper it is more likely than not that you will find that you would be the loser. The figures you would be given to review would take into consideration the income you might realize from the investment of the money you'd receive, the interest you would be paying on the combined balance of the old mortgage and the new one, the taxes you could deduct for the interest you would be paying, the taxes you would pay on the income you would be getting, and, finally, the monthly payments you would be making compared with your present monthly mortgage payments.

In most cases an offer of the type illustrated has the homeowner giving up the remaining 10 years of mortgage payments in exchange for 30 years of mortgage payments at twice the number of dollars per month. It would be unusual to be able to recover that difference with the income produced by investing the borrowed money.

Paying off the old mortgage. At the time of retirement many couples living in a home or condominium with a number of years of mortgage payments ahead think that it might be a good idea to get rid of the mortgage payment monthly expense. The answer is easily arrived at. How does the interest rate on your existing mortgage compare with what you can earn, or are earning, with the money it would take to pay off the mortgage? If you have a 7 percent mortgage, for example, and can have your money in a money market fund earning more than 7 percent, it would be a mistake to terminate the mortgage. Throughout the inflation years young people have been advised that the best investment they could make was to buy a home with a long mortgage. They not only would have reason to expect an increasing value but, in addition, they would be paying off the loan with cheaper and cheaper dollars. It was good advice. For as long as you are in a situation where you can earn more than you can save it is not good business to pay off the mortgage

Selling your home. Perhaps you will decide to sell your home. You may reach that decision because the home is too big for you now, because maintaining it has become far too expensive, because the neighborhood is going downhill and you no longer feel safe about the environment or about the falling value of your property, or because you elect to transport yourself to another part of the country or the world. All are valid reasons.

Anyone, at any age, gets a tax break upon the sale of a home that properly can be called one's *principal residence*. Your principal residence can be a conventional home, a condominium or co-op apartment, a mobile home, a boat, a hand built log cabin in the woods. It doesn't matter. All that counts is that it is the place where you have spent most of your time — your real home. IRS doesn't say that it had to be your real home for any stated period of time. The tax break is that no matter how much profit there may be in the sale, you pay no tax on it provided that you buy another home within two years and that you pay as much or more than you received. You cannot just buy the new residence, you must be living in it within the 24 month limitation. You can do this as often as you please.

At age 55 and thereafter you get another tax-free privilege but once only. When you sell your home, as much as $125,000 of profit is completely free of tax. Any profit over $125,000 is subject to the usual but favorable capital gains tax. To be entitled to the $125,000 tax exemption, the home you sell must have been your principal residence for at least three of the last five years. It need not have been three years in succession, just a total of three out of five.

Being able to pocket as much as $125,000 of profit plus the original cost of your home gives you an income producing base that can be an important help in your next move, whether it be a purchase or rental. But, perhaps you won't be in a position to make the sale to anyone with that much cash. You may not be able to find anyone who can raise enough cash for a down payment or can get the needed loan. You may find that your best move is to rent your home until conditions are more favorable to making the sale.

Renting... there are some dangers. If you are not careful you could lose your right to the $125,000 of tax-free profit when you sell. Keep in mind that you are entitled to that exemption if the home was your principal residence in any three of the past five years. Renting your home for too long a period could rule out that important tax break unless, after the rental period, you move back and remain in the home long enough to qualify.

You could also lose your right to defer any capital gains tax by putting the proceeds of the sale into the purchase of another home within 24 months. If you rent your home for more than one year Internal Revenue will treat it as an investment and won't permit the tax avoidance when you sell.

Renting brings with it certain tax advantages. You may deduct from the rental income you report all of the interest you pay on mortgage payments, depreciation, repairs, maintenance, property taxes, fire and liability insurance premiums, real estate agent's fees and utility bills not paid by the tenant. You may also deduct the cost of any redecorating or repairs you contracted for to make your home easier to rent. None of these tax deductions may be taken unless you rent. Major additions and renovations are not deductible expenses. They do add to the basic cost of the home, however, and therefore reduce any capital gain tax when you sell.

Helping a buyer to finance the purchase. An interested buyer with a good credit background and income that is sufficient in relation to what the monthly payments may be, could have trouble getting the necessary mortgage loan. There is more demand than there is a supply of dollars available from the traditional lenders. If you are satisfied that the potential buyer is a sound credit risk, it might pay to entertain the idea of being the lender. Do not rely on your unsupported judgment or your sense of the person's quality. With the help of your bank, your lawyer, your real estate agent, your accountant — one or several of them — make a thorough investigation before you agree to finance the purchase.

Second mortgages. The more usual way for a homeowner to ease the financial problems of a buyer is to agree to accept a second mortgage. The buyer, for example, has been to a savings and loan association that is willing to provide the major loan on a first mortgage but requires that the buyer give you a down payment of $20,000. Your buyer needs $10,000 more than he can raise at the moment. You, having done your checking, agree to accept half of the down payment in cash and the other half in the form of a second mortgage. You must be certain that the terms of the first mortgage permit the existance of a second mortgage.

Second mortgages involve more risk than first mortgages. It is called a first mortgage because it comes first in case of trouble. If the buyer cannot keep up with the mortgage payments and there is a foreclosure, the first mortgage holder collects everything coming to him before you can collect a penny. It is customary, therefore, for the interest on a second mortgage to be a few points higher than the first mortgage commands. If the laws of your state bar you from asking as much interest as the higher risk suggests you can compensate for that by increasing the selling price sufficiently to make up the difference.

Selling your home in this manner gives you whatever cash is paid as down payment and a flow of monthly income representing a very high yield on that portion of the down payment you did not collect in cash.

The first mortgage. Holding the first mortgage is not done as frequently but it has its advantages. Were you to sell your home in the usual manner, where the buyer gets his financing from his bank or thrift institution, you would be paid all cash and you would look for ways to put that money to work where it would supply you with a flow of income to pay rent on your new dwelling and for other purposes. Taking the first mortgage gives you the high yield mortgage loans are commanding, and it also gives you a gradual return of principal — the paying off of the loan — over a long period of years. You have the protection of being able to reclaim your home should the purchaser get into financial difficulties.

Installment sales. If the capital gain amounts to a good deal more than the tax-free $125,000 you can handle the transaction as an *installment sale.*

Installment sales, to be recognized as such by Internal Revenue, are simply sales where an agreement has been made that payment will be made in more than one tax year. When you sell and are the holder of the first mortgage the transaction will be treated by IRS as an installment sale unless you claim all of the gain in the year in which you make the sale. Where the gain is $125,000 or less, assuming you are age 55 or older, this would be the thing to do. But if the gain exceeds $125,000, an installment sale may reduce your taxes.

Installment sales serve to spread the gain over a period of years. When you are able to do that you customarily reduce the amount of tax you'll have to pay. Installment payments received over a number of years would consist of three elements: some would be a tax-free return of capital (the repayment of the cost of your home), some would be interest and some would be capital gain. Just 40 percent of the profit exceeding the tax-free portion is taxed. You pay your normal top tax rate on that amount. If your top bracket is 30 percent, the tax on $50,000 of profit would amount to $6,000 (40% of $50,000 = $20,000. 30% tax on $20,000 = $6,000).

An outright sale would put all of the gain in a single

year, increasing your top tax bracket and, consequently, subjecting all other income to a greater tax in that year.

Remaining in your home. Refinancing and the sale/leaseback ideas offer ways to stay in your home while capturing some of the equity to supplement your income.

There is another way of solving the problem created when you are intent on holding on to your home but are income short. Here is a story that tells the story:

Life Estate Agreement. Marty and Martha Grew live in a home they bought some years ago for $60,000. They have a mortgage on the home calling for payments of $430 a month. They still owe $20,000 on the mortgage. Although Marty, at age 66, is retired from his former position, he is acting as a consultant and earns about $18,000 a year. In addition, the Grews have investments that produce another $8,000 of annual income. Because of his consultant fees Marty has no Social Security benefits yet, and probably won't have before his 72nd birthday. They are not in financial trouble, but they find that inflation is forcing them to lower their living standards. They no longer can take the vacations they both enjoyed. The nature of their meals reflects the times — more vegetable and pasta dinners than ever before. These and other changes in their living style are taking some of the pleasure out of life. They decided to take action.

The first thing they did was to put on paper all their major expenditures. They were not surprised to see that two of the bigger ones were income taxes and the mortgage payments. Recalling something he had read some months back, Marty visited the Salvation Army. He said, "My wife and I may be interested in donating our home to the Army if we can continue to live in it for as long as either of us lives. Is it possible?"

"It certainly is," he was told. "That is called a Life Estate Agreement."

"What about our mortgage?" Marty asked. "We still owe $20,000 on it and the monthly payments are $430. Will you take over those payments?"

"That won't be necessary," the Salvation Army officer told him. "To start with, since the interest rate you pay must be considerably lower than present interest rates, whoever holds your mortgage probably wouldn't permit anyone else to assume it. Here's what we'll do. We will buy your home for the $20,000 owed on the mortgage. You can use that money to pay it off. IRS considers that arrangement a *bargain sale* and we are careful to abide by IRS regulations so that you don't lose any of the tax advantages you are entitled to."

Marty asked, "Does that mean that I no longer will pay real estate taxes on the house?"

"No," he was told, "it doesn't. The property will pass to the Army by means of a *Warranty Deed* which will carry the provision that you and Mrs. Grew retain the right to live in your home for as long as either of you lives, after which the property passes to the Army. You will, in addition, have to give us a letter stating that you will be responsible for the upkeep of the property, regular maintenance, heat and water bills and the payment of real estate taxes. But your federal income tax will be reduced. You will be entitled to a substantial deduction for a charitable contribution. The amount you may deduct is based on the current market value of your home, less the $20,000 we will pay you. That figure will be reduced by depreciation on your home — not on the ground, of course, but on the house — and finally on what is called your *remainder interest*. Remainder interest amounts to the value of the right to live in the house for the duration of your lives. That is arrived at by applying your life expectancies to an Internal Revenue Service formula. Don't let me make this sound too discouraging. Based on my experience with quite a number of these arrangements, I estimate that your deduction will be in the area of $50,000.

"When you fill out your income tax report you will be allowed to deduct as much as 30 percent of all your taxable income by that amount. Since you probably cannot take full advantage of the $50,000 in one year, you may take similar deductions annually for as long as five additional years or until you have used all of it. Not only will your tax payments be substantially smaller for those years, the deductions will drop you down to a lower tax bracket. That's an additional advantage."

The arrangement gave Marty and Martha a galaxy of benefits. They no longer had to pay $430 a month for the mortgage. For a period of years their taxes were greatly reduced. They no longer had reason to worry about having to move from their home. And, as an unexpected bonus, the home would not be subject to the expense of a probate, which generally amounts to about 8 percent — a very worthwhile saving, considering the value of the home.

That is one way of solving income problems with the *life estate agreement.* If the Grews were in the same situation but their home was free and clear — no mortgage — the same arrangement could have been made. This time, since there would be no mortgage to pay off, the $20,000 would have been invested to produce income for them. The figure of $20,000, of course, is purely hypothetical. Depending on the market value of the home, it could be a lot more or it could be less. The cash portion of the transaction will, of course, influence the size of the permissable deduction.

A charitable remainder trust. As amazing as it sounds it may pay to give your home away. You would donate it to a legitimate charity, university, hospital or some like organization registered with the Internal Revenue Service as a non-profit organization under Section 170(c) of the Internal Revenue Code. The chances are that just about any potential recipient of that type, that you have any interest in, is properly registered.

Once again, to clarify and to bring to life what would take place, here is an illustrative story: Art and Mable Gyver live in a big home they bought more than 40 years ago. They raised four children in that home, saw three of them married in the big front parlor, and today Art and Mable live there alone. They actually use about one-third of the house but they pay to heat and maintain all of it. The cost of doing so has become a severe burden and, despite all of the memories and sentiment attached to the old home, they want out. Their four children are all married. Three of them have given Art and Mable grandchildren they rarely see, for the young families are scattered all around the nation.

What the Gyvers have decided to do is to sell the home and to find small rental apartments, which they will take one year at a time, in each of the localities where their children now live. No more anchors for them.

Their problem is that the home they bought for $18,000 more than four decades ago sits on a full acre in an increasingly desireable part of a growing city. They can sell for more than $300,000. $125,000 of the profit would be tax-free but even though they would have favorable capital gains treatment on the rest, they are distressed at the way the proceeds of the sale will be reduced by the combination of federal and state taxes. They want all the income they can manage to get so they will be able to enjoy their remaining years and not have reason to worry about financial matters.

They presented the problem to their next door neighbor, Bert Tillman, a well regarded financial planner. It was Bert's idea that they should not sell the home but should give it away. In going along with his suggestion, and guided all the way by him, these were the steps taken and the results.

1. They arranged with Art's old university to donate the home through a *charitable remainder trust.* The university, having investigated, established the fact that the home had a realistic value of $340,000 and that several real estate developers were eager to buy. The donation was made and the university sold the property. Since the Gyvers gave and did not sell, they had no tax liability.

2. Before turning the property over the Gyvers were told that they were to make a choice. The university would create either an Annuity Trust or a Unitrust for them. Bert advised them to take the Unitrust. "The difference," he explained, "is that an Annuity Trust will provide you with a monthly income check for as long as either one of you lives. The amount of the monthly payments will never change. The Unitrust is different in that the monthly payments *will* vary. Now this is the important consideration," Bert said. "You are going to receive income on the full market value of your old home — $340,000. Not one penny will be subtracted for taxes or anything else. Whether you choose the Annuity Trust or the Unitrust, the $340,000 is to be invested in a group of securities that will be continuously supervised by investment professionals. The university, taking your ages into consideration, will determine what your income will be. It probably will be 10 percent or better. That means that the Annuity Trust would give you $34,000 a year for the rest of your lives. If you elect the Unitrust you'll get the same income the first year but each succeeding year your income will be based on 10 percent of *whatever the value of the securities* *happens to be.* If you two believe, as I do, that inflation will continue and that a carefully supervised and selected investment in high quality common stocks will mean growth of value and income, you will see why I prefer the Unitrust. It is capable of giving you cost of living increases." And that was their choice.

3. The charitable remainder trust also has the significant advantage of giving the Gyvers tax deductions they can enjoy each year for six years. They may take deductions that will reduce their taxable income by 30 percent each of those years or until the allowable deduction is all taken.

4. When both Art and Mabel are gone the payments end. That is when the university takes the home and has no obligation to the Gyvers' estate.

The decision must be made whether to take this step or to bypass it for the reason that it does not allow for any part of the value of the home to be inherited by the children and grandchildren. And that, of course, is a highly individual decision.

The illustration of how the Gyvers adapted the charitable remainder trust to their ideas and needs does not mean that you will use it in exactly the same way. The trust, for example, can have as many different options as commercial annuity contracts offer, as detailed on page 70. It is a flexible technique well worth exploring if you think it might serve your purposes.

There are a number of technical aspects to the setting up of the charitable remainder trust. Some of the major charities, universities and hospitals, have experts familiar with what is needed. They will handle these matters without cost to you. Before making a final choice of which institution to favor with your donation, it is a good idea to ask them how well equipped they are to establish the trust.

Your next home. Jess and Jessica Jameson, in retirement, have sold their home for $130,000 and the $125,000 tax-free gain privilege more than took care of the profit they realized. The decision to sell was based, in part, on their having found a considerably smaller home in a quiet suburban area that suited their needs admirably. The new home was offered to them for $100,000. They studied their alternatives carefully.

No matter what they did, they saw an urgent need to increase their income. If they bought the new home for all cash, that would leave them close to $30,000 to be invested. If they made a $24,000 down payment and took a long term mortgage the monthly payments would be about $1,000 a month and there would be real estate taxes as well.

Conservatively, they decided that they should not rely on being able to realize more than 10 percent on their capital over any extended period of years. After subtracting the down payment from the proceeds of the sale of their old home there would not be enough capital to produce the income needed for the monthly mortgage payments.

They found their solution by making a mutually rewarding business deal with their son and daughter-in-law, David and Terry. David, a dentist, had a well established practice. Jess and Jessica explained the situation to them. Jess said, "You share our enthusiasm for the new home we have our eyes on and I know you agree that there is ample reason to believe that it will grow in value as the years go by. What we propose is that you two buy it and rent it to us. Here is how we suggest that be done. A $24,000 down payment is required. We are going to give each of you a gift of $12,000 — the $24,000 needed. As you probably know, IRS permits each of us to make gifts of $10,000 to each of as many people as we please without involving any gift tax — the *annual exclusion.* As a couple we can give each of you as much as $20,000 in any year free of gift tax. By making those tax free gifts to you we can put the $24,000 needed for the down payment in your hands painlessly.

"You will buy the house and we will rent from you. Your costs will be about $1,000 a month. David, I recall your telling me that your top tax bracket is close to 50 percent. For a number of years the great bulk of the monthly payments will be for interest, which is tax deductable, so your out-of-pocket monthly costs for mortgage payments will be about $500. You'll also have real estate taxes to pay. We will pay you a monthly rent of $600."

David and Terry were delighted. They were buying a property for three quarters of the sales price; the rental income, although taxable, would enable them to handle the balance of the purchase at a bargain rate; and they had an investment that was likely to keep growing in value. Jess and Jessica had what they wanted. They would have the home they wanted. They would have approximately $100,000 to invest. At 10 percent yield they would have $10,000 a year — almost $3,000 more than their rental payments.

Vacation homes as income producers. The opportunities to use a vacation home at the shore, in the mountains or elsewhere, for a combination of fun and profit are strictly limited. If you rent the home you are allowed to take as deductions against the rent you collect only mortgage interest and property taxes that are greater than the total you collect. Should your income from rent be greater than all expenses, however, you do better. In that case you may deduct your costs for utilities, repairs, insurance, depreciation, mortgage interest and real estate taxes. You may not, however, apply any loss against other income.

The good news is that if you, family or friends, do not use the home for more than 14 days a year, or for 10 percent of the days the home is actually rented at fair rental value, you do not have to report rental income at all. On the other hand, you may not deduct any expenses other than mortgage interest and taxes.

The one other thing you may do about an investment in a vacation home is to make no personal use of it but have it strictly as a business investment, renting it out as much as you can. Under those circumstances you are allowed to deduct all expenses against income, including depreciation. It is a way of acquiring a vacation home for income, for future use, or for eventual sale at a profit, with little or no cost. If all costs in any year exceed rental income that loss may be used to reduce other reportable income. If you fail to show a profit in two out of five years, however, IRS can take the position that what you have is a hobby and not a business and your loss claim will be rejected.

Mortgage investments and limited partnerships

Investing in second mortgages. With home prices towering and mortgage loan rates sharing those dizzy heights, home buyers are hard pressed to find the dollars needed to purchase homes and real estate people are equally hard pressed in their efforts to consummate sales. The people who want to put their capital in second mortgage loans, therefore, will find that there is a rich supply of welcome mats. Investing in second mortgages can give you an excellent yield and good profits but it is also a high risk way of putting money to work.

The same elements that make second mortgage money sought after — high prices and the high costs of borrowing — create considerable danger for the second mortgage investor. The burdens on the home buyer are heavy. If they become too heavy, you could be in trouble. The holder of the first mortgage comes first and you, the holder of a second mortgage, come second if the buyer falls behind. If a home is foreclosed, you get what's left, if anything, after the first mortgage people collect what is theirs. In a market where real estate values are increasing, there is an excellent chance that a foreclosure will lead to a sale that will take care of everyone and even leave something over for the one who owned the home. But there are no guarantees that this will happen. The economy and real estate values can turn down, and a foreclosure could leave you in a very poor situation. On the other side of the coin, since the risks are high, so are the rewards. The average life of a second mortgage is from five to ten years and, as a rule, the second mortgage investor buys the mortgage at a discount of about 5 percent for each year the loan is to run. On a $5,000 five year second mortgage, for example, you actually put out just $3,750. You collect the prevailing rate of mortgage interest on $5,000 and at the end of the five year period you collect $5,000. The average second mortgage involves monthly payments of interest only. The $5,000 comes due in a lump sum at the end of the term. It is a very inviting investment but check and double check. How financially sound is the borrower? If he *seems* to be financially sound why did he have to resort to a costly second mortgage?

Ginnie Mae and Freddie Mac mortgage investments. Those are the well established nicknames for two government sponsored routes to mortgage investing. Ginnie Mae refers to the *Government National Mortgage Association* and Freddie Mac is the playful term for the *Federal Home Loan Mortgage Corporation.* They were created to make more mortgage loan money available to the public. Through Ginnie Mae certain organizations, meeting their requirements, are enabled to issue securities backed by pools of FHA and Veterans Administration mortgages. The firms issuing the securities collect the mortgage payments and the payments are paid out to the investors. The payments are guaranteed by the government, whether the home owners do or don't meet their mortgage obligations. In addition to that, the yield on the Ginnie Mae securities are right in step with current mortgage rates. As an investor you have high yield and a beautiful absence of risk.

Freddie Mac is a U.S. government corporation. It puts together pools of conventional mortgages. Here, too, the mortgage payments are passed along to the investors. While the payments are not guaranteed directly by the government, they *are* guaranteed by an agency of the U.S. government, Federal Home Loan Corporation, which makes them safe but there are many who put more faith in the government's direct guarantee available in the Ginnie Maes.

There are three things that take away from the appeal of Ginnie Mae and Freddie Mac. Number one is that they are available in $100,000 denominations only. (Don't run away...there is an answer to that.) Number two is that you could have capital gains and you could have capital losses from these investments. At this writing the yield on these securities is in the neighborhood of 15 percent. Two years ago, had you invested in either one of them, the yield would have been around 7 percent. These are long term investments since mortgages, as you know, generally run for 20 or 30 years. If you owned a 7 percent Ginnie Mae at a time when new Ginnie Maes were paying 14 percent you would face a most substantial loss were you to sell out. You would have to give a new investor a big enough discount to give him a 14 percent yield or better. If you paid $100,000 you would have to sell for about $50,000. On the other hand, it could work the other way around. Buy one that now pays 14 percent and just possibly, two years from now, new issues might be all the way back to 7 percent. In that case you could sell at a handsome profit.

The third negative is a bit involved and it also brings to light one more advantage you could enjoy as an investor. The average life of a 30 year Freddie Mac, for instance, is more like 12 years. That is because people owning homes whose mortgages are in that Freddie Mac pool move, die, cannot keep up with payments and are foreclosed, or they sell. When any of these things happen the mortgage is paid off and the proceeds are distributed to you and the other investors. That is the plus, for in addition to the high yield you also get a flow of extra dollars as these events occur. The trouble is that you have to get involved with very complicated record keeping; you have to know what to report as income and what to report as capital gains and what is tax-free return of capital. You must keep up with the record keeping or you will have a king-size problem if you ever want to sell. Without accurate records you will not know exactly what you are offering for sale. The security you bought has changed. At the time when you first bought there might have been as many as 500 mortgages in the pool. By the time you sell that figure could be much smaller. If you are to ask a broker to sell for you, he must know what it is he is selling, and it would be up to you to give him that information. If you are a meticulous record keeper and can handle the complexity of something of this nature, all well and good. Otherwise, you have a severe headache.

Happily, at this writing, there are two mutual funds invested exclusively in Ginnie Maes: Lexington GNMA Income Fund (if you want their literature and prospectus you can use their toll free number, 800—526-4791) and Vanguard Fixed Income Securities Fund, GNMA Portfolio (800-523-7910). Lexington requires a minimum investment of $1,000 and Vanguard's minimum is $3,000. Both of them do all of the required record keeping and you get a tax-time statement telling you what part of your income was ordinary income, what part was a tax-free return of capital and what part was long term capital gains. As with all other mutual funds, they stand ready to re-purchase your shares on request, so you have no liquidity problems. They buy and sell the pooled securities in which they have investments, which means that your yield is not frozen and the management of the funds do a professional job of watching the market and acting in a continuing effort to avoid losses and to realize profits. In addition to these two specialized mutual funds, many of the money market funds and high-grade bond funds have Ginnie Mae and Freddie Mac issues as parts of their portfolios of securities.

You may be wondering what a mutual fund is doing in the real estate field, for that is where Ginnie Maes and Freddie Macs live. Just appreciate the fact that mutual funds provide a *method* of investing, a method that can be employed in a great variety of ways.

Real Estate Investment Trusts (REIT). Although REITs (pronounced: *reet*) are not mutual funds, they have many of the same features. REITs have a number of different real estate investments, reducing investment risk. At least 90 percent of all income and profits must, by law, be distributed to shareholders and usually it is 100 percent. The big dollars normally associated with real estate investments do not bar people of average means since the shares are offered in reasonably small denominations. There is continuing professional management. In each of those areas they do mirror mutual funds. Unlike mutual funds, they do not offer to buy back your shares. This, generally, is not a handicap for REIT shares are readily bought and sold through investment dealers. There are three types of REITs:

1. The *equity REIT* is a package of apartment houses, office buildings, shopping centers, warehouses and such. The total concentration is on owning income producing properties. Not only do the properties create income for the investors, but management tries to produce profits

through the advantageous sale of some of its holdings when the proper opportunities present themselves. An equity REIT uses part of its revenues to reduce mortgages on its properties. As the debt decreases the value of the holdings increase. Another marked difference between a REIT investment as opposed to a securities investment is that the REIT shareholders, in addition to the earned income received, also enjoy income resulting from depreciation management takes on the properties.

2. *Mortgage REITS.* There are two kinds. One invests in short-term construction and development loans and the other deals in the long-term financing of large projects such as apartments, and office buildings. The income produced by the interest charged on the loans are passed through to the shareholders as are any profits or losses that may result from assignment of loans to others, foreclosures and other events.

3. *Combination REITs.* By dealing in the ownership of properties as well as short-term and long-term lending for real estate projects, the combination REITs are in a position to alter their investments in keeping with economic changes.

The laws under which REITs operate do not permit them to actively manage or finance their own projects. These vital functions are handled by management/advisors under contract. The experience and integrity of the managers are of extreme importance to you as a potential investor.

Because real estate values have advanced so much over recent years, REITs, for the most part, have been good producers of income and profits. This has been particularly true of the equity REITs for obvious reasons. The greatest benefit REITs offer is that, attractive as real estate investing has been, most people do not have the money, knowledge and expertise to invest in real estate projects on their own. REITs provide ways of overcoming those obstacles.

Real estate limited partnerships. On page 87 of Chapter 3, real estate limited partnerships were introduced. You saw that these constitute the only way present tax laws permit you to have the dollars you and the other limited partners invest multiplied many times over by money borrowed *without your having any liability for the repayment of the loans.* At the same time, you are permitted to take full advantage of the borrowed money in that you can take tax deductions based on the gross investment and you can realize income and profits produced by the gross investment.

That is called *leveraging* — the use of borrowed funds to amplify your opportunities for profit. Were you responsible for the repayment of the loans, you would be leveraging your chances for profits *and for losses.* A non-recourse loan removes the threat of leveraged losses. One reason why it is possible for a real estate limited partnership to borrow money on a non-recourse basis is that the real estate that is part of the project is security enough for the lenders.

Real estate limited partnerships give you some of the same benefits to be found in REITs. They offer a chance for you to be involved in sizeable real estate projects without requiring you have great sums of money and they relieve you of the need to be an experienced, knowledgeable real estate person.

There are two types of limited partnerships. There are the very big ones, sometimes called *syndications*, where the money brought together by the partners and bank loans may be spread over many different big projects. These are registered with the Securities and

Exchange Commission and you must be provided with a prospectus that has been filed with SEC before you invest. The syndications are sold by investment dealers. Some are originated by the larger New York Stock Exchange firms. The other type of real estate limited partnership is called a *private placement*. In most cases private placements are a good deal smaller than the syndications and only a small number of partners may participate. The usual top limit is 35. Many are formed with one general partner and just two, three or four limited partners. The private placements can be organized for the development of just one project, for the acquisition of an existing building, a shopping mall, or what have you, or it can have a goodly number of properties.

The minimum you may invest for the average syndication is $5,000. Private placements generally require a lot more. Some, however, allow you to spread the investment over a period time.

Some people prefer the big syndications. They reduce risk because, as a rule, more properties are in the package. Being registered with SEC gives many investors increased confidence and it may be said that their greater resources permit them to employ more and better qualified real estate investment and management experts — a debatable point. Those who favor the private placements contend that they get a better deal. Little or nothing is spent on promoting sales of the limited partnership units; overhead is less; legal costs and accounting fees are lower because they can avoid the complexities of full registration. They are not free of supervision and the need to abide by rules and regulations, however. Before investing, have a lawyer, accountant or financial planner, well versed in real estate, investigate the general partners, their backgrounds, their track records and the specific project or projects contemplated.

Frequently the big syndications will sell limited partnership units to create what is known as a *blind pool*. That is when the general partners do not buy any properties or land or start any developments until all of the participation units have been sold. The contention is that the real estate market is too changeable for them to negotiate before they are in a position to close deals, which they cannot do without money. Blind pools are not necessarily more risky than offerings that are based on precise properties and projects, but it does pose a problem for a potential investor to make a judgment as to the income and profit potential.

The great appeal of both types of real estate limited partnerships are:

1. In the early years there are large tax losses from depreciation, mortgage interest, expenses, etc. These losses are passed on to the partners who may deduct them from income from other sources. There may be some cash distributions which are considered to be return of capital and, therefore, tax-free.
2. Long term capital gains can be anticipated through the combination of growing values and the gradual reduction of mortgage indebtedness.
3. Thanks to the non-recourse loans, which usually are substantial, the limited partners enjoy both tax deductions and tax sheltered income far in excess of what they would have had without the benefit of leverage.
4. The partners have no responsibility for the partnership's borrowings.

These are not risk free. Bad management, excessive vacancies, bad legal work that could lead to a denial of some of the expected tax advantages — any and all of these could create losses in excess of income *and* tax advantages. One other disadvantage is the problems you may have if you want to sell your units before the partnership ends. The average life is eight years. That, however, may be less of a risk than it has been with existence of the Liquidity Fund described on page 88.

Just as syndications are offered by investment dealers, so too are some private placements. Others may be brought to your attention by financial planners, real estate developers, accountants or attorneys.

Since the outstanding benefits are tax losses and tax sheltered income, unless you are in the 50 percent tax bracket the chances are that this is not a suitable investment for you.

Real estate investments

Investing in real estate on your own, if you are retired or are approaching that time of life, raises a number of questions. Are you in a position to invest a fairly large amount of capital? Are you able and willing to have the capital tied up for an extended period of time? How much risk can you handle? How much knowledge and experience do you have to support decisions involving a real estate investment?

Raw land. Of all possible investments in real estate raw land is least likely to be appropriate for those in or near to retirement. In addition to the original capital needed to make the purchase, it costs money in terms of ongoing real estate taxes. Another consideration is the income lost by tying up your money in a non-income producing investment. Generally it takes a number of years for a raw land investment to mature to the point where you can sell out and realize enough profit to make up for all the costs. The experts say that raw land has to increase in value 20 percent a year to make it a good investment. There are exceptions. If you should happen to stumble on the opportunity to buy undeveloped land at a low price at a time when the area in which it is located happens to be in the path of a major development you could do extremely well. The question is, are you in a position to find such an opportunity before the full-time real estate professionals will? Maybe yes. Probably no.

Commercial real estate investments. More often than not the amount of capital needed is substantial. The risks are high. When vacancies occur they may be difficult to fill. If there are drastic changes in a neighborhood, which can happen with particular speed in a commercial area, the value of your property can take a severe beating. On the other hand, it is an income-producing investment and commercial leases can be longer and more elastic than those for dwellings. It is not out of the ordinary to have a lease that runs for 10 or 20 years which embraces automatic increases — based on changes in the cost of living, increases in real estate taxes — or based on a percentage of the occupant's sales.

A commercial real estate investment need not be on a big scale. You can invest, for example, in as modest a venture as a small retail store. How successful you will be depends, to a great extent, on how thoroughly you investigate the location. Is it on the way up or on the way down? If you learn of things taking place that suggest that the area is becoming more desirable, then you must be certain that the zoning is right for your visualization of the best uses for the property. You could, for example, study a neighborhood and conclude that there is no restaurant within a reasonable distance and that the property you are interested in would be ideal for that purpose. Can a restaurant opening there get a liquor license? There could be a number of reasons why the application might be rejected. If that proves to be true, no restaurant operator is likely to be interested.

To spare yourself problems and unexpected expenses, consider renting your property on what is called a *net lease*. That type of lease may require you to reduce the rent somewhat but the tenant assumes all of the problems and costs of maintenance, other than responsibility for the exterior of the building. You have to take care of the roof and anything else on the outside. The tenant shoulders all inside repairs, replacements, heat, air conditioning and all other utilities.

The tax deductions you may take increase your net income. If you spend money improving the building, and the structure is at least 20 years old, you may take a 10 percent tax credit for whatever you spend. You will deduct all interest on any money you borrow for the purchase. Taxes are deductible and you have depreciation deductions.

Depreciation can be looked at as a *cost-free expense*. You don't spend anything but you take deductions as though you did. That, of course, increases the amount of money you keep after taxes. To make that still more appealing, the probabilities are that the true market value of your property will be increasing year after year while you are enjoying deductions based on a decreasing value. There are a number of ways of taking depreciation. You accountant will guide you to whichever system fits your situation most advantageously.

Residential investments. If you enjoy rolling up your sleeves and working on a house and are good at it — if you team up with someone who has that aptitude — investing in individual residences can be rewarding. Finding good buys is not easy — the demand for housing is so high that undervalued homes are few and far between. To successfully buy, rehabilitate and sell a home, you should know how to judge the soundness of a building. Your greatest opportunities will lie in the finding of a home or homes that are in disrepair, look delapidated, but are structurally sound. These are the ones you can take over and redeem. With hard work, good taste and the investment of some capital over and above the purchase price, you can bring about magical change, making the shunned, run-down dwelling excitingly appealing. The price you will get when you sell or rent will reflect what you have achieved.

From the tax standpoint it is important to know what is deductible and what is not. *Repairs* may be deducted; *improvements* may not. However, whatever you spend on improvements may be added to what you paid for the building and that will reduce the taxable gain when you sell.

Chapter Seven

Real Estate and Retirement — Do They Mix?

RICHARD WOLLACK *has earned a national reputation as one of the most innovative and successful marketers of real estate investment projects. He has been a featured speaker at national financial forums and a frequent contributor to the financial press. Having known and admired his brilliance for a number of years I asked him if he would turn his thoughts to real estate for people in retirement. He chose the question and answer format to express his very sound ideas.*

Q. *My husband and I are near retirement age and we were thinking of buying a small apartment building rather than investing in real estate with someone else. We would live in one of the units and manage it ourselves. Does this make sense?*

A. Your idea of investing in and managing a small apartment project could be a fulfilling and financially rewarding approach. Although there are many investment considerations, generally speaking managing the

177

property yourself can give you an *active* retirement. Nonetheless, before undertaking such a venture you should carefully consider the following:

1. Make sure your temperament is such that you would enjoy managing an apartment complex. The time demands and people interaction problems of managing even a small apartment complex can be significant. You should assess your own personality to determine if you are prepared for such a challenge.

2. Make sure that you're not putting a disproportionate share of your total assets into one property. The lack of diversification is a significant factor to consider.

3. A great many people have similar capabilities or intentions as you have, therefore, the opportunity to find an attractive investment is difficult. The market demand for 6, 8 or 16 unit apartment complexes is quite extensive. In many parts of the country it is nearly impossible to purchase such a property with a positive cash flow, despite what the real estate broker's "fact" sheet might indicate.

4. Be certain you have sufficient reserves to allow for unplanned necessities such as a new roof, boiler or air conditioning unit, etc. All of these (and dozens more) can wipe out cash flow and, in many cases, produce a significant negative cash flow for the entire year on a small property.

Consider the idea of postponing the purchase of a property immediately. Attempt, instead, to find a job as an apartment manager in the same market and on the same type of property you anticipate buying. There will be nothing more illuminating as to whether or not managing a property is a long-term situation you would enjoy. Also it will give you valuable experience as to the realities related to owning and managing such a complex. After a year you should have a very good feel for both the property's economics and its ability to provide you the economic return you are looking for. You'll also have more time to look for a reasonable investment.

Q. *For someone contemplating retirement, what types of real estate investments appear best?*

A. The answer to that question, of course, depends on various personal financial circumstances. In general, many individuals who ordinarily would look to invest their retirement dollars in long-term, fixed interest rate assets have been putting part of their cash into real estate investments to provide a hedge against inflation. Depending on retirement age, an individual may not want to take quite the same risks or need quite the same tax benefits. People who are younger tend to invest in real estate which produces more tax benefits through the use of significant leverage — adding borrowed money to their own investment — with the acceptance of somewhat greater risk. In retirement, people generally desire a higher rate of cash flow, greater stability and preservation of capital. This can be achieved through several different real estate investment alternatives.

One good strategy is co-invest in some of the new pooled investment programs. These have been created especially for pension and profit sharing plans, but are suitable for individuals in retirement. Through them you can invest in real estate purchased on an "all-cash" or low leverage basis. These produce a much higher current return and less tax benefits than leveraged transactions. But because they are unleveraged they safely maintain a direct hedge against inflation, albeit not as great a profit potential. An investor in this type of program could anticipate increasing cash flow over the years as well as potential profit upon the conclusion of the investment program. It is a combination that can help to maintain purchasing power.

Another approach that is becoming more popular is the use of REITs or limited partnerships which lend money on properties and, in some cases, participate in the increasing revenues or profits from those properties on which they lend. These investments provide a high level of current cash flow and the possibility of profits. There are typically little or no tax benefits associated with these investments.

A third approach is to seek an investment program created by some sponsors in which the benefits of ownership are split between different groups of investors — one seeking higher levels of current cash flow and another group who desire the tax benefits and growth. These are typically called "A-B" programs since they create two classes of investors. The "A" (income) investor, receives a preferred return from the real estate investment and may share in a small portion of the appreciation. The "B" (growth) investor receives all of the tax benefits and the majority of the growth. A final approach is an investment in second mortgages or second trust deeds. This real estate investment does not produce any inflationary hedge, but merely a high level of current income. These are typically short term, fixed rate investments and produce no upside potential or tax benefits.

Q. *Upon retirement we're thinking of keeping our home up north, renting it out, and either buying or renting a condominium in Florida to retire in. What do you think?*

A. I assume the rationale for keeping the home up north and renting it out is either due to a personal desire to maintain some ties up north or the belief that the home is an asset which will continue to appreciate. As for the first motivation, if you feel you want to maintain the residence for family or personal reasons, by all means do so. Understand, however, that when you move to a state like Florida (which does not have an inheritance tax) for your retirement, keeping your northern home might subject you to your home state's inheritance tax. If, instead, you sold the property and bought another residence in Florida you would minimize inheritance taxes. Also, even though you might sell your northern home, you should have little or no capital gain to be paid on the sale of your older home, even if you do not buy a new one, since people over the age of 55 get a one-time capital gain exclusion of $125,000 on the sale of their residence.

Maintaining the home up north merely as an investment, and living in the south year round may not be the wisest approach. You are not taking advantage of the important capital gain exclusion and homes generally do not receive a rental sufficient to produce substantial return on the true equity in the home. Hence, you might be better off selling the home and investing your substantial equity in an alternative real estate investment. In that way, you could have higher income and an equal inflationary hedge. On top of that you will avoid all of the management headaches of absentee ownership. Being an out-of-town owner is quite time consuming and costly when owning just one small property.

Q. *We have a number of investments in real estate limited partnerships and were wondering how we might go about liquidating them early. We have a need for the cash for other purposes.*

A. Since real estate limited partnerships are non-liquid by their nature you should not invest in such a program if you contemplate a need for the capital sooner than the investment's sponsor is planning to sell the property. But given your desire to liquidate you should generally recognize that you will not be able to receive the full current value of your share of the real estate because anyone acquiring your units will want some discount for taking over your non-liquidity. With that in mind, in most limited partnerships, the best course of action is to contact the general partners and inquire what services they might provide you. Alternatively, you might contact the securities dealer, if any, who might have sold you the transaction. Both can often assist you in the liquidation of units by finding other potential buyers who may have indicated an interest in acquiring units of the program(s) you are in. Alternatively, you might consider contacting Liquidity Fund (415-652-1462), a San Francisco area based company which buys units of most limited partnerships, both publicly and privately offered. They will evaluate your units and make an offer based upon the current value. Oftentimes, investors receive well in excess of their original investment. Of course, you may personally seek out individuals you know to inquire about their interest in purchasing the units. If you do sell, you will generally get a higher price the longer your investment program has been in existence. The more successful the real estate investments have been, the higher the current cash flow and the shorter the length of time anticipated for the properties to be held. Naturally, you will be offered something less than what the investment is worth, but the value of becoming liquid is often worth the discount, especially if you are still making a profit. Finally, you might consider selling the investment yourself to a third party.

Q. *I am contemplating a real estate investment, but I wonder about the lack of liquidity, given the fact that I'm entering my retirement years. Am I unduly concerned?*

A. Your general concern for real estate's lack of liquidity is not unwarranted. No one investing in a real estate program should even contemplate needing the capital during the life of the investment. However, your concern could be undue, depending on your circumstances. Typically, investors desire to have a very high portion of their assets in liquid investments. In fact, the chances of ever needing all of one's assets in readily liquid form is quite remote. By requiring complete liquidity an investor is foregoing the increased potential returns available from investments which have less liquidity. One of the reasons that real estate traditionally out-performs other types of more liquid investments (such as stocks, bonds, etc.) is the fact that the investment marketplace generally rewards individuals who are willing to accept a liquidity risk — the risk of *needing* the capital upon short notice — not the risk of *losing* the capital. Individuals who are able to accept this liquidity risk for at least a portion of their investments are able to enjoy higher returns. The simplest example of this phenomenon would be the purchase of a bank certificate of deposit rather than putting your money in a passbook account at the same bank. The safety of principal (or "business risk") is identical, yet because an investor is willing to wait for the return of his capital (i.e., he accepts a "liquidity risk") by investing in the CD, he receives a significantly greater return. So too, with real estate. The fact that many investors shy away from real estate because of its lack of liquidity is the very reason why those people who do invest in real estate generally can expect a higher rate of return. Consequently, you should be asking yourself what portion of your capital you can afford to put into relatively less liquid investments in order to obtain significantly higher return. If your assets are modest, the percentage in real estate may only be appropriate in the neighborhood of 5%-10%. For investors with large net worths, the percentage of investments in less liquid items can approach 30%-50%. Of course, even real estate investments should have a program of eventual liquidation and you should time your investments so that not all of them come due at the same time, but provide you a continuing roll-over of funds.

Chapter Eight

The Time of Transition

When retirement time arrives what changes, if any, should be weighed? What changes should be made in your financial affairs? Are there universal *musts*? Are there some alterations in one's savings, investments, wills, insurance, banking, home ownership, tax handling, forms of registration, degree of liquidity, risk vs. safety and record keeping that demand immediate review and possible change?

Because of the importance of these considerations, and because they involve a variety of areas calling for specialized knowledge, I invited a group of outstanding people to meet with me for a roundtable discussion.

Meet the individuals who, through the pages of this book, serve as your advisors as you cease being an active earner and start being a retiree. In alphabetical order, they are:

Dr. Edmund Fitzpatrick, Director of the Industry Consortium for Retirement Planning, National Council

On The Aging — *General Robert N. Ginsburgh*, Neville Associates, Financial Planner — *Harry J. Lister*, CFP, Executive Vice-President, Washington Mutual Investors Fund and a member of the Board of Regents of The College For Financial Planning — *Charles Thomas Martin*, Certified Financial Planner, Senior Vice-President, DeRand Financial Consulting and President, Washington, D.C. Chapter, International Association of Financial Planners — *Stephen A. Nauheim*, attorney, Anderson, Hibey, Nauheim and Blair, formerly an assistant Branch Chief in the Internal Revenue Service Chief Counsel's Office — *August Zinsser III*, Senior Vice-President, Trust Officer, First American Bank of Washington.

The exchange of ideas was handled by my tossing out a series of provocative thoughts and whoever had an observation to contribute said his piece.

***We started by talking about the advisability of simplifying one's financial affairs so that if travel is to be a major activity in retirement, for example, everything is in order and under control — and an added measure of relaxation could be enjoyed during the leisure years.*

Attorney Nauheim: In the effort to simplify financial affairs in retirement there may be the impulse to consolidate securities holdings — to reduce the number of issues held. Before making the initial moves the tax considerations must be given careful study. Some very complicated tax planning could be needed to get over that first hurdle or there could be a big and needlessly heavy tax bite.

Planner Martin: It seems to me that there really should be no sudden changes at retirement. In most cases there is no reason why the changes should not have been handled over the years on a gradual basis in preparation for retirement. Normally people know from three to five years in advance what is going to happen to them. Tax planning and income planning should be in place by the time of retirement, so that you can go off to wherever you want to go and relax. There are people, however, who just at the time they retire start thinking, "Now I have to change everything." I had a call Tuesday from a man who was retiring on Thursday and moving to Saudi Arabia. He suddenly realized he had some problems — what sort of military benefits he should take and a long list of other things.

If people will start to plan and take some actions long enough before retirement, say at age 50 or 55, they have the opportunity to start moving some of their assets. They may decide that they have to convert all of their assets to income vehicles since they will no longer be working. Fine. They'll have a couple of years to see how this is working and they may decide that maybe they can't retire and should keep on working. That is less traumatic than going into retirement and then finding that their planning wasn't practical; it doesn't work. The transition, in other words, should be gradual.

Banker Zinsser: Many of the people I see don't plan. They retire and they panic. They feel that they now face a very complex situation. That is how they see it. Usually it is not complex nor is there any hurry about making changes. Nothing says they have to make changes right away. The transition should be slow and steady, not something that occurs overnight.

Attorney Nauheim: Another facet of this is that there are some people who do some sophisticated advance planning and then, for any number of reasons, are faced with the need to retire years before they had expected. Some of these people, particularly those in high tax brackets, may be in various tax-sheltered investments that produce no income. They find themselves in a situation that doesn't fit their economic needs at that time. Disposing of tax-sheltered investments can be painful since the early year's tax deferrals are typically payable at the time of disposition. The ideal, of course, is to find an investment that will generate substantial tax write-offs in the years of high income and high tax bracket, and a steady flow of income in the later, theoretically lower tax bracket retirement years. Rental real estate and oil and gas can provide this combination but a potential investor must be *extremely* careful to be sure he is buying a high quality product.

Dr. Fitzpatrick: So often people facing retirement look closely at their financial situations for the first time. Prior to this, they most likely had not studied the personal benefits statements provided by their employers nor inventoried their personal assets. With retirement on the horizon, they start to inquire about investments, wills, trusts, etc. — and with all of this information coming at once, things appear immensely complicated. They wonder how they can make good decisions. They see a need to uncomplicate things so they can make decisions they understand and can feel comfortable with, and which will serve their objectives. The basic issue, though, is not whether their affairs are too complicated, but how to gain an adequate understanding of the wise and unwise financial alternatives available to them.

***The next subject brought up was the matter of changing the nature of any securities investments; whether there is wisdom in moving from growth situations to the pursuit of pure income; or total return; and if holdings that provide some tax shelter should be continued or is it something they no longer can afford.

Planner Martin: It isn't unusual today for a retired person to have as much as thirty years to live; a very long time. Those years must be financed. Unless the husband or wife, or a single individual is an expert in dealing with finance this can be a very complex and difficult problem, particularly in a period of inflation. I'm just pointing out that longevity is an important consideration.

Planner Ginsburgh: I think it is particularly important for the person to look at his or her own situation from the standpoint of what income is needed, what the tax implications are and how long he may live. People used to think that when you retire you must turn everything from growth to income. But if you are going to live another 20 to 30 years you had better have some growth as well as income. Today, when so many people retire and have retirement programs, it is imperative that they look into those programs — those annuities — to see whether or not they have cost of living increases built into them or not. What they discover should dictate what proportion of their assets should be concentrated on income and what part should be concentrated on growth. Similarly, we used to figure that most people were in a lower income tax bracket after retirement but that isn't necessarily so. For those in retirement who are in fairly high tax brackets, it might well be that they have excellent use for some tax shelters.

Banker Zinsser: I say "amen" to that. If you are going to live a good number of years you better have a lot of growth built in. If you have a solid retirement plan that you can depend on, paying you a stated amount, or one that changes with the cost of living, you should look at that as a form of fixed income return. Do that and you give yourself more opportunity to get into growth investments than if you ignored it. You should not try to balance off your securities on an income versus growth basis, ignoring your retirement annuity.

Fund Executive Lister: One of the things I've observed quite often is that when people reach retirement they feel that they have to reapportion some of their assets. They believe that they have to switch from common stocks to bonds, or in some way increase their income producing assets, not realizing that they will continue to need growth and may now use some of their growth oriented investments in an income-producing mode. Systematic withdrawal programs, for example, may provide them with the cash flow they need with the asset they currently own, and still allow for long-term appreciation potential. Although this desirable feature is advertised and described in mutual fund prospectuses and the funds' other literature, by the time the person who has had common stock fund investments for a number of years reaches retirement this feature is often forgotten.

Dr. Fitzpatrick: I conduct a one-day financial planning seminar for people considering retirement and I have them develop a portfolio for different types of people. One will be for someone who has just become a widow, one for a person just retired under one circumstance, and for others who have just retired under different circumstances. What I have found in doing this is that they are very sensitive to the emotional needs of the individuals and they are willing to take more risk now. They are alert to growth and to what inflation means. Because of inflation they want growth built into their retirement investment plans, and they are willing to accept more risk to get it. These are average company employees but they are attuned to financial realities, which indicates to me that more and more of them will recognize their own limitations and will be more inclined to seek the help of, and will be better able to understand, professional financial planners.

Planner Martin: One of the things that should be pointed out is that when people do retire and start to take a retirement benefit that many times the money they draw in the early years may be a refund of their contributions that they paid into those plans. They may have 50 percent, 60 or even 80 percent of their salary continued for the next year or so that will be tax-free to them. That gives them a planning opportunity. If they do have to make some changes, or if they want to make some changes later, they can take those capital gains now and not worry about the impact of making some changes from a tax standpoint. That's a built-in tax shelter. They don't have to try to create some tax deductions in some other manner.

***Invasion of capital was brought into the discussion at this point, whether this was a healthy thing to do, or something to avoid.

Banker Zinsser: I think it all has to do with what you are invading capital for. You build up your capital in one way or another, with or without the help of your employer and real estate or securities investments and then, at retirement, you decide you want to make a change and it requires the invasion of capital. I think you should go ahead and do it. If, however, you live off your capital, reducing it on the assumption that your life expectancy is fifteen years and you live beyond that point the invasion of capital can be a self-defeating proposition.

Planner Ginsburgh: I think it is preferable to invade *capital gains* than it is to invade capital. That may be a very useful way of getting you the kind of income you need to live on at a lower tax rate. You are taking into account total return. One of the best ways to invade capital is through a systematic withdrawal program. Just be sure that if the life expectancy tables say you are going to live another fifteen years that you withdraw on the basis that you'll live another twenty or twenty-five years.

Dr. Fitzpatrick: I've noticed an interesting attitude on the part of many, if not the great majority of pre-retirees on this question. I saw an article in a popular magazine recently that reported the same phenomenen. Specifically, many pre-retirees believe they would rather spend all of their money while they are living instead of leaving it for their children and their estates. The question with them is not whether to invade capital, but how fast to invade it. They are playing the guessing game... how long am I going to live?

Planner Ginsburgh: On the other hand, those same people who say they want to spend it all while they live know they're not going to. When you talk to them about doing some estate planning so they they can leave, say, an additional $30,000 to their children, instead of to Uncle Sam, this gives the issue a different perspective.

Fund Executive Lister: One of the most useful tools in this area is an annuity contract which is, obviously, an invasion of capital. One way in which that annuity contract can be very attractive is when it is used to accumulate and tax defer earnings in order to begin a regular income distribution when you reach a more advanced age, let us say, seventy-five. At that stage you may convert all or a portion of your assets in the annuity policy for the rate of return... total return, now... which at such age is very high. The annuity company believes you don't have many years remaining so if you outguess them it can be very rewarding. If the company thinks you have ten years and your family history shows that you should have fifteen or twenty, that type of contract at this point in your life can prove to be a very valuable investment.

***Liquidity and control were introduced for discussion...the considerations that might be brought to bear on long and short-term investments, the dangers of being locked in, and kindred problems.

Planner Martin: Just because they have retired does not mean that people need complete liquidity, particularly where there are benefits coming from a retirement plan. The retirement plan can be considered the fixed portion of one's investments. Unless they have specific needs for liquidity, like that big trip, the purchase of a retirement home, or whatever, I don't see why liquidity should suddenly become a great problem. Any major purchase, such as selling their home and buying another, or *keeping* their home and buying another, could call for the liquidation of some securities and such. Otherwise there should not be any sudden motivation to be totally liquid. As long as total return is adequate there need be no change in long-term or short-term liquidity needs. As far as being locked-in to some investments, if they can be locked-in to a high yielding debt security at a time when the prime is twenty-five, that presents the opportunity to have a very high total return when the prime comes down and they can sell the security for a fine capital gain. I cringe at the thought that someone might say, "I am now sixty-five and I have to radically change everything I am doing." That is panic. They panic because they are not aware of the alternatives.

Attorney Nauheim: Often, the best form of liquidity is borrowing, using "locked-in" investments, such as real estate, as security for the loan. The borrower avoids any tax results and his investment continues to work for him. Private pension plans, particularly those of closely held companies, where the plans are more likely to be tailored to the needs of individuals, can be an attractive source of this type of liquidity.

***The question of risk. When a person stops earning money and will be living on interest, dividends and capital gains, should there be a change in attitude as to the degree of risk they are willing to take?*

Banker Zinsser: The change should not be radically different, but there is one thing they should bear in mind. The loss they might take while they are working can be recaptured with earnings. After they are no longer earning and are living up to, or nearly up to, their annuity and retirement income, losses probably cannot be replaced. That doesn't mean, though, that there should be a sudden, radical reaction. But you see a lot of people who do this. They do it in either of one or two forms, either of which is equally bad. One group rushes out at retirement and buys the highest return they can get . . . a 30 years bond at an increasing discount. Or they convert everything to cash and buy a six-month money market certificate of deposit. If their timing is good they hit the peaks in interest rates. If it is bad they hit the valleys and they have done themselves a disservice. Both are extremes, but you see an awful lot of extremes; either total liquidity, total savings or total investment for total return . . . all extremes.

Fund Executive Lister: In this area we have to look at the considerations that come up when weighing rolling over a lump-sum distribution from a qualified retirement plan. Understanding the pros and cons is extremely important. If the amount coming out of the plan in under $20,000 there probably will be no tax at all. The tax factor gets larger as the distribution gets larger. If the amount of the distribution and the tax liability are not too great the wiser course may be to take the distribution in cash and put it to work in an appropriate investment other than an IRA rollover.

Attorney Nauheim: Add to that the fact that income averaging can reduce the tax to the point where not enough is gained by the rollover.

Planner Ginsburgh: That is extremely important. What we are talking about is not just 10 year forward income averaging. Of particular importance in deciding whether to take the lump sum so that the retiree may use income averaging is what lies ahead. If you make the assumption that the individual is going to live for 10 years or so, on analysis, you'll find that you are not likely to beat the benefits with a rollover. This is true even where fairly large sums are involved.

Attorney Nauheim: On the other hand, if investments can be made *within* a qualified plan rather than with proceeds distributed from the plan, the income that will result will not be taxed as long as it is retained in the plan. In some cases this can amount to an effective doubling of the return on your investment.

****Insurance is a subject that raises a number of questions at the time of retirement.*

Planner Ginsburgh: In most cases any disability insurance will be discontinued, since its purpose is to replace earnings if a person becomes ill or injured. While working, it is more important than life insurance. When your primary income shifts from earnings to income from investments, Social Security, annuities and other retirement sources, you probably don't need that kind of protection.

Banker Zinsser: Group term insurance programs provide a step-down conversion. It reduces the protection to a lesser amount in most cases. The problem is that people had that insurance as protection against premature death. If you still feel you need it after retirement, the conversion being quite costly, you are gambling that you won't outlive the cost of carrying it.

Planner Martin: In retirement the one type of insurance that is vital is protection against huge medical expense. Without it you can be wiped out.

Dr. Fitzpatrick: For the couple without an adequate nest egg or income protection for a survivor, life insurance can be the means to an instant nest egg for the survivor. Most people, as they approach retirement, are probably "mis-insured", but are unaware of it. They haven't focused on the problem yet, or don't know what to do about it.

***Home ownership demands attention. The value may have gone up considerably and could be an answer if you are capital short. If there is still a mortgage you have another set of problems. Since it is the largest asset many people have it justifies a good deal of inspection.

Dr. Fitzpatrick: The problems and opportunities are diverse. A home may represent a substantial potential capital gain, and one question that should be faced is, will it keep its value if, for instance, illness results in improper maintenance?

Banker Zinsser: At retirement many people switch from one residence to another. Some or all of the gain can be deferred if the home is sold and another bought.

Planner Ginsburgh: The age is a major factor there. After age 55 you pay no tax on as much as $125,000 of gain. If you switch to a smaller home, or a retirement home, because it will cost less to maintain, you must look ahead to what the annual expenses may be. Those costs can skyrocket, as indeed they have in recent years, and eat up current income you were counting on.

Attorney Nauheim: One aspect that needs watching when you have or buy a second home, say one in the north for the warm part of the year and one in the south for the winter months, is which is your principal residence? This could create a real problem. Only the principal residence can qualify for the tax-favored rollover treatment. Keep in mind also that the up to $125,000 of tax-free gain is available only one time.

Fund Executive Lister: Financial planning involving the home can become difficult because of psychological factors. It is where the family was raised, the garden grown. It is the comfortable, well-loved anchor. It often is hard to look at figures and say, "We'll sell our home."

Dr. Fitzpatrick: The old family home can represent a severe financial burden. The home that was purchased years ago for $30,000 and is now worth $50,000 may be burdened with utility bills of $300 a month and the taxes can be crushing. It may be wise to sell the home and use part of the proceeds to buy a smaller, new energy-efficient home that requires little maintenance. At the same time, the tax-free gain of up to $125,000 can be put to work generating more retirement income.

Chapter Nine

Other Ways of Investing

Money can be put to work in countless ways. So far we have looked at many different types of securities, annuities, Keogh and IRA, a few tax shelters and a variety of real estate investments. There are still more roads to travel.

As inflation has become more and more of a problem in recent years, the search for ways to fight it has brought considerable attention to a variety of *non-income producing areas of investment*. Propelled by concern over shrinking buying power of the dollar, great numbers of people look for places to put their capital where they hope it will be *inflation-proof*. There has been no shortage of new businesses emerging to cater to those urgent desires. Starting in the early seventies, an army of merchants offering ways to invest in gold, silver, diamonds, rare coins, art, rugs and a variety of other "beat inflation" opportunities, have aggressively promoted their wares. Some are sound and legitimate. Many are not.

Retired people who need all of the income they can get have absolutely no reason to become involved with any of these investments. They produce no income. On the contrary, they involve expense. None of them are even intended for quick profits, but are for those who are prepared to see their investment grow in value — they hope — over a period of no less than three years.

For those who have ample income and want to put a portion of their capital where it appears to have a good chance of riding with or surpassing inflation, one or more of the following concepts merit review.

Gold

Gold has been a revered medium of exchange for more than three thousand years. It is appealing to the eye, it is in short supply, and it has an impressive history of keeping its value in line with inflation. Those are the positive facts. There are negatives, particularly for people in retirement.

The biggest negatives are these. It produces no income. It can be expensive to hold, for it must be stored and insured, and there may be a need to pay to have it assayed (appraised to determine the purity of the gold) before buying or selling. It is highly speculative, for although it has kept pace with inflation *when given enough time*, there have been long periods when gold prices were falling while the cost of living was rising.

The fact that it produces no income can be its most serious shortcoming if earnings have ceased and you depend on your capital to give you the spending money you need. Obviously, an investment that costs and does not pay is not going to serve your needs unless it can produce a sizeable profit for you within a reasonably short period of time. Your dependence on that possibility is reckless speculation.

Paul Volcker, Chairman of the Federal Reserve

Board has made this comment: "The discipline of gold works only if nobody changes the price. Once you admit that the same men who print money in effect 'print the price of gold', all you have done is to find a new way of printing paper money." In other words, the price of gold's dizzy swings are, to a great extent, the outcome of government actions. At the same time, governments have the deciding voices in currancy valuations. And it isn't just governments who can, unexpectedly, bring about dramatic differences in the price of gold. Edward Hipps, a Dallas coin dealer, put it this way: "Someone like David Rockefeller could sink $1 billion into gold now and the price would jump tremendously. This is a big game for big people, and the little fellow has to guess right to play." Proof of that is what happened to the price of silver when the Hunt brothers put a huge fortune into it and then were compelled to retreat. No yo-yo ever moved up and down faster — and a lot of innocent silver investors were hurt. In the past forty years, the price of gold has gone from $35 an ounce to $850; and down again to less than $400.

Still there are those who firmly hold to the idea that putting some portion of their capital in gold is desireable insurance against the possibility of dollars becoming worthless.

If you have all the income needed to live the life you want to live and believe in giving yourself some *golden insurance*, there are several choices open to you. These are the most popular:

1. *Gold bullion.* Bullion — solid pieces of gold — comes in sizes that vary from 400 ounce bars, or ingots, down to wafers that weigh less than an ounce. The price you pay, as is true with so many things, gets lower as the amount you buy gets higher. The lowest prices are paid by those who purchase lots of five or more of the 400 ounce ingots. At $400 an ounce, five ingots would cost

$800,000. On top of the purchase price you must add the cost of storage, insurance, and assaying.

There are alternatives. At least four organizations, Deak-Perera in Washington, D.C., Dreyfus Gold Deposits, Inc., Citibank, and Republic National Bank — all three in New York City — will sell you Gold Certificates. You own the bullion but you do not take possession. You get a paper certifying that the specific number of ounces of gold you purchased is being held in storage for you. You are relieved of the concern for its safekeeping, transportation, quality and the eventual sale. You can arrange for its sale with a phone call. You actually sell the Certificate. Minimum purchases range from $1,000 to $2,500, and the charges are from one percent to three percent.

2. *Krugerrands.* The South African Krugerrand is a gold coin that weighs exactly one troy ounce. A troy ounce is the traditional standard for weighing gold. More American citizens own gold in the form of Krugerrands than in any other form. The coins are easy to store, to buy and to sell. They usually sell for about five percent above daily value of the gold they contain. One prominent precious metals dealer says that Krugerrands are so convenient and reliable that anyone buying less than $100,000 worth of gold will do well to confine the purchase to these well accepted coins. To find out where to buy or sell Krugerrands in your vicinity, you can make a toll-free phone call to 800/257-7880; in New Jersey, 800/322-8650.

3. *Gold stocks.* This is one way of putting some of your capital in gold that pays dividends. There are U.S., Canadian, and, of course, South African gold mining stocks. South Africa is the source of most of the world's gold. Some of these stocks pay spectacular dividends and offer the possibility of capital gains. Be aware, however, that your investment in South African stocks

brings with it the normal investing risks plus the possibility of serious political upheaval in that country.

One other way of investing in gold stocks is through some mutual funds which invest primarily in gold bullion and/or gold stocks. Two of these are International Investors, Incorporated, whose shares are sold by investment dealers, and Golconda Investors, a no-load fund, at 11 Hanover Square, New York, N.Y. 10005.

4. *Commodity futures.* You can buy futures contracts for gold, silver, platinum, other precious metals, and agricultural products. They are extremely speculative. When you buy a futures contract, it gives you the right to buy a specified amount of gold, or what-have-you, on a certain date at a certain price. You pay between five and ten percent of the value of the contract, plus a sales commission. Your hope is that by the time the date arrives the product will be worth more than the price you agreed to pay. If it is worth more, you have a profit. If it is worth less, your contract is worthless and you have lost everything you paid.

Diamonds

The word *diamonds* comes from the Greek word, *adamas*, meaning invincible. Many of the organizations currently promoting investments in diamonds, as a means of beating inflation, project the image of those glittering gems as the invincible answer. Some of their arguments are telling. Here are a few:

1. Diamonds are the most concentrated form of wealth known. One ounce can be worth close to a million dollars, compared with the $400 or $500 value of an ounce of gold.
2. They are almost industructible.
3. Demand is growing and the supply is shrinking.

4. Prices are controlled by a profit-orientated international organization resulting in annual increases in value.

The last item is particularly interesting. Seventy-five percent of all rough diamonds come from the Soviet Union, South Africa and Zaire. Eighty-five percent of all newly mined rough diamonds are channelled through, and are under the control of the Central Selling Organization, a London based organization controlled by DeBeers Consolidated Mines. They regulate the supply going to the world markets. They regulate the prices, adjusting them for inflation, to ensure a steady increase in value. The price control is unique. Since the beginning of this century the value of diamonds has trended upwards, with extremely few deviations. There have been no severe drops, as have been witnessed in the value of gold and silver.

The companies that have emerged to promote diamonds as the inflation fighting investment for today have gone to great lengths to invite confidence. It is evident that buying diamonds with any degree of confidence constitutes a challenge to the average individual who is ill equipped to judge quality. Chief among the attributes the diamond investment companies set forth is that the diamonds offered are graded, certified, identified and insured. Laser and other highly sophisticated techniques are employed in the process. No two diamonds are identical. Some companies go so far as to encase each diamond sold in a sealed plastic container along with an identifying number related to a laboratory report — all of which is insured as to identity by Lloyds of London, or some other well established insurer. The second confidence appeal is the seller's guarantee to repurchase the diamonds.

Some of the larger, longer established companies featuring diamonds for investment suggest that you

make the investment only if you will not have need for the invested capital for three to five years.

Historically, diamond prices have been increasing, over an extended period of time, by about fifteen percent a year. Those who have a sceptical view of diamonds as an investment point out that investors buy at retail and are paid at wholesale when they sell. That, they state, is why it is necessary to wait at least three years to break even. The additional consideration is that your investment earns nothing for you throughout the waiting period — you have lost whatever the money could have been earning in a money market fund, for instance. On the other hand, the profits made when the diamonds are sold are subject to the favorable capital gains tax, a maximum of 20 percent — as opposed to ordinary income tax on investment income, a maximum of 50 percent.

If diamond investing appeals to you, be extremely selective about the company you choose. Learn all you can about it. Examine their track record, particularly for repurchases. Query the Better Business Bureau about them. Study with great care how the diamonds are graded, certified, identified and insured. In checking their repurchase agreement, be certain that all fees and charges are made clear so that you know how they arrived at the net sum you will be paid.

Rare Coins

Investing in rare coins has become quite popular. There is a good deal of romance and interest involved over and above opportunities for profit. The hobby appeal, the speculative aspect of any gold and silver content, and the history of growing value make rare coins particularly attractive. Over the past twenty years the average annual growth in value of top quality rare coins has averaged 20 percent a year. Over the past five years the rate has averaged 28.7 percent a year.

Some who believe that they have *buying power insurance* when holding gold and silver prefer to make their investments in rare coins. They reason that any strong dips in precious metal values will have far less impact on their coins, simply because of the numismatic value of the coins themselves. On the other hand, there are many valuable rare coins that contain no precious metals at all. They are made of nickel, copper or other lower cost metals. Krugerrands and similar coins are bought and sold on the basis of their gold content. They are not rare coins and, thus, have no numismatic value. The factors that make rare coins valuable are:

- Rarity — how many were minted in any given year
- Excellence of condition

Rarity can be deceptive. It is natural to confuse rarity with antiquity. In 1976, for example, a very small number of $100 gold pieces were minted in the Bahamas. Because so few were put into circulation, they are worth a good deal more than most Roman coins that were minted 1700 years earlier. So many of the Roman coins were produced that, even today, they are available in relative abundance.

As is true of diamonds, one must be expert to select rare coins for investment. If you lack the knowledge and training which would qualify you as an expert, there are quite a few companies ready and willing to act for you. New England Rare Coin Galleries of Boston, for example, claim to have the largest group of numismatic experts in the world and a multi-million dollar inventory of rare coins. One way of investing that they suggest is a monthly program of acquisition. You can invest as little as $100 a month. Each month their staff will select and send you various coins they consider to be of good investment quality. Along with the coins, they include certificates guaranteeing the grading and the

authenticity. As your safeguard against ever finding that any coin purchased from them is counterfeit, they certify that in such a case they will refund the purchase price plus twenty percent compound interest for each year you have had the coin. When you want to sell, they will repurchase your coins "at the same grade," or will put them up for sale at the frequent rare coin auctions they conduct.

The rare coin dealers counsel that you should not plan on investing if you are not prepared to hold your coins for five to seven years, for you will be buying at retail and selling at wholesale, and it takes time to overcome that difference and give you a profit.

Rare coins can make rather spectacular price moves up or down, making it a fairly high risk investment unless you are planning to hold your investment over a considerable period of time. One example of how prices are influenced was discussed by a prominent coin dealer. He pointed out that most coin dealers carry inventories of rare coins and of gold bullion and silver, as well. "When gold went from $850 an ounce down to $400 an ounce," he said, "we were paying record interest charges to hold our bullion until prices recovered. In the meantime, we were forced to sell coins to cover our losses." Forced sales create reduced prices.

Collectibles

The term *collectibles* is applied to many things that people collect for pleasure or for profit. Stamps, Chinese ceramics, petrified wood, paintings, statuary, rugs, antique jewelry, colored gem stones, rare books, autographs...the list is long. Inflation has motivated many people to put their dollars in collectibles in the belief that prices were rising at a clip that would beat the rising cost of living.

I was profoundly shocked while watching a television interview with two of the financial editors of one of the country's most respected new magazines. They were conducting a "how to beat inflation" session with a studio audience. One woman in the audience asked, "My husband and I have $1,500 in a savings account earning so little. Should we keep it there?"

A member of the magazine team replied, "No. Take that money and go to a flea market. Pick out something old that's in good condition. You'll be able to sell it later at a good profit."

What an incredible piece of advice to give to someone concerned about income, who has given no indication, whatsoever, that she knows beans about antiques or art! The editor would have counseled better had she told the poor woman to take the $1,500 and blow it on a good time.

Just about all collectibles are sold by experts to non-experts. The experts are in the business to make money — and not for you. Burton Malkiel, Chairman of the Department of Economics at Princeton, and a member of the President's Board of Economic Advisors, made this observation, "Collectibles are far more overpriced than real estate, and the transaction costs are enormous."

Collectibles can be profitable if you thoroughly understand whatever you are investing in; if you know the values; if you know that you are dealing with people of unquestionable integrity; if you know that you can find buyers when you want to sell; if you can afford to tie up your money in a non-income producing manner for a relatively long period of time. If you can nod your head to all of those qualifications perhaps you will make a profit if conditions, beyond your control, don't drive the values down.

All-Saver Certificates
The Reagan tax-cut measures introduced something

new; tax-exempt savings certificates you can buy in $500 denominations from banks or savings and loan institutions. The certificates will yield 70 percent of the average yield of one-year Treasury bills. Those rates change each month. Whatever rate is in effect when you buy your certificate will be your rate for the full year life of the certificate. Presently the all-saver certificates are to be available only through 1982, but this could change.

An individual may buy as many of the certificates as he or she pleases but the maximum amount of interest that will be tax-free is $1,000, or $2,000 for a couple filing a joint return.

Withdrawal of the money you invest prior to the one-year term is expensive. You will lose both the tax exemption and three months of interest.

If your top tax bracket is 30 percent or greater it is a good investment. If it is less than 30 percent you can do better putting your money where it earns as much or more than Treasury bills are paying at the time you are contemplating the investment. For example; if the certificate pays 15 percent and you are in a top tax bracket of 25 percent your tax-free interest would be equal to a *taxable yield* of 14 percent. Therefore, if you put your money in a money market fund, for instance, paying 16 or 17 percent, you are better off. The higher your tax bracket the more attractive the all-saver certificates are.

Cash Management Account

Merrill Lynch has a financial service that inspired *Fortune Magazine* to say, "The Merrill Lynch Cash Management Account may be the most important financial innovation in years." If that prediction proves to be accurate, the probability is that by the time you read this, a number of other brokerage firms will be promoting look-alike services.

The *cash management account* is offered to securities investors as a means of making maximum use of every bit of your invested capital with total ease, convenience and efficiency. You open an account with Merrill Lynch with $20,000 or more in cash, securities, or other assets, or a combination of money and assets. The money is invested in securities selected by you with the help and guidance of your Merrill Lynch broker. The cash management account gives you five special services:

1. All idle funds — money not invested, or dividends, interest and any realized profits — are promptly invested in their money market account or their equivalent of a tax-free municipal bond trust.
2. You can write checks against your account.
3. You are given a line of credit based on the value of your securities.
4. You are given a special VISA card you can use internationally.
5. You get a monthly statement showing your securities holdings, checks that have cleared and VISA charges that have been paid out of your account.

This novel service comes close to the long heralded *one-stop financial service* that brokerage houses, banks and insurance companies have been anticipating for years. It can have particular interest for people in retirement who want to travel and not worry about day-to-day financial decisions and record-keeping; for people who are ill and want relief from dealing with financial matters; and for people who just have more peace of mind if they can put most of their financial affairs into competent hands other than their own.

Chapter Ten

Protecting What You Have

Everything we have covered thus far has concentrated on ways to have more capital and more income in the retirement years. The final thing you should consider is how to protect whatever assets you have or will accumulate — how to protect against needless taxes that are unrelated to income and profits — how to protect those family members who are to be your heirs.

Inheritance taxes — also called estate taxes — have generally played a big part in financial planning. Nobody liked the idea of working hard to accumulate capital knowing that a major portion of it would go to the tax collector instead of to wives, husbands, children and other family members. With the tax cuts that were enacted in 1981, that is much less of an issue. By 1987 there will be no Federal inheritance tax if you are married, even if you are a millionaire. If you are single, you still can own as much as $600,000, and there will be no Federal tax. State taxes, if any, may or may not be a problem. The states have their individual rules, rates and regulations. It is a good idea to learn what estate taxes are in your state. If they constitute a threat, you may want to plan actions that may help to sidestep some and possibly all of them. Some low cost life insurance may be your best answer.

Until January 1, 1982, Federal inheritance taxes came into play if your taxable estate amounted to $175,625 or more. The Reagan tax cut greatly increased the tax-free portion of one's taxable estate. On a graduating basis the tax-free amounts are: in 1982 — $225,000; in 1983 — $275,000; in 1984 — $325,000; in 1985 — $400,000; in 1986 — $500,000; and in 1987 — $600,000. In addition, a married person may pass on to his or her mate $250,000, or half of all assets, *whichever is the greater*, without that portion being included in the taxable estate. That means that in 1987, if married, you could have as much as $1,200,000 and escape all Federal inheritance (estate) taxes. That is certainly good news and it will continue to be good news until, and if, high rates of inflation make a million dollars no more than a modest estate. Should that happen, the Congress may, once again, boost the portion that will be tax-free. Right now, Federal estate taxes pose a problem only for the very wealthy.

Gift taxes have been eased by the 1981 tax cuts too. Until the new legislation was passed you had an *annual exclusion* from the payment of gift taxes on gifts of $3,000, and you could make those $3,000 annual gifts to as many different people as you pleased. No gift tax. Now the limitless number of free gifts can amount to $10,000 each, and if man and wife pool their exclusions they can give $20,000 each year to each of their children, to each of their grandchildren and to any number of nephews, nieces, cousins, neighbors and so on. No tax.

The annual exclusion is particularly welcome to those who enjoy spreading their wealth while they can witness the enjoyment of it — and it is a splendid way of avoiding the heavy costs of probate which could come up if the money were to be given by means of a will. Probate, the process of every detail being examined by the Probate Court, involves expense and time delays, and it can also lead to unwelcome publicity because Probate Court records are open to the press and the public. The cost of probate averages around eight percent. If it can be avoided it should be, but probate is not all bad. When a will is subjected to probate, it means that the interests of your beneficiaries are examined by a judicial process and that all of the assets involved are properly inventoried and evaluated. If your estate is not complicated and you have more capital than you need, you can save your inheritors time and money by making gifts while still living.

Wills. The human tendency is to avoid thinking and doing anything about unpleasant subjects. That, plus superstition and plain carelessness must be the reasons why eight out of ten people die without ever having had a will. Nine out of ten financially successful people die with wills that are so out of date that they create severe problems for the survivors.

The simple fact is that if you fail to have a will, all of the assets you have worked so hard to accumulate will be disposed of in accordance with the laws of the state where you live. The chances of the law distributing your possessions in the manner you would have chosen are not very good.

If you see the desirability of *your* deciding what should be done with what is yours, instead of leaving those decisions to total strangers, run to the nearest lawyer and provide yourself with a will. You should have one and your husband or wife should have one. Don't put it off because you think that it may cost too much. Any lawyer will tell you in advance what the fee will be. A fairly common figure is $50 to $150 for a simple will.

If you have a will, how long has it been since you reviewed it? Wills should be read and up-dated with a fair degree of frequency. Changes in the family — births, deaths, serious illness, weddings, divorces, hard feelings, and the patching up of hard feelings — these, plus changes in your financial situation and other factors, can make changes in your will important. If you sincerely want to protect those you leave behind, don't postpone the writing or up-dating of your will. Take action now.

Joint ownership. It is commonplace for people to assume that if the home and any investments and bank accounts are registered as joint ownerships there is no need for a will. If one partner dies the other inherits everything automatically. That is possible, but it can also create a situation that is seriously in conflict with what you want to happen.

What follows are just a few of the reasons why jointly registered property may be an inadequate way of disposing of your assets in keeping with your wishes:

1. A man and wife perish in an automobile accident. It is determined that the wife outlived her husband by an hour or two — or even by a matter of minutes. When the couple married the man was a widower and there are two minor children from his first marriage. The laws of the state where the couple lived requires that all of the assets must go to the nearest relative of the *last survivor* — if there is no will containing contrary instructions. As a result, the well loved children get nothing and the proceeds of the estate go to a nephew of the wife, whom she has not seen or heard from for more than thirty years.

2. The survivor may not have the knowledge, experience or the mental capacity to handle

money. A carefully up-dated will can take these circumstances into consideration and can contain detailed instructions as to who should be responsible for handling the assets in a manner that will protect the survivor. Joint ownership, without such a will, would not... could not... make such provisions.

3. Without a will there is no way in which the joint registration of bank accounts, real estate and securities can cover everything, nor are there any carefully thought out provisions for handling of final expenses and taxes. The absence of such arrangements can be costly.

Finally, when you do have wills, be sure that they are prepared by and in the possession of your lawyer, not locked away in a safe-deposit box or a desk drawer where locating them can create some severe problems.

Life insurance. During one's earning years and throughout the period when a young family is growing, when minor children are being supported, life insurance is absolutely irreplaceable. It is the one means of giving yourself an instant estate that would not exist otherwise. It is the one means of protecting the family from economic disaster if the principal earner should prematurely die.

In retirement the considerations are totally different. By that time of life there are not likely to be minor children. There is no need to develop a replacement for earnings. The income you are receiving in retirement, while it may be reduced, will not come to a screeching halt as do earnings when the earner is removed from the scene.

One of the key reasons why many people have maintained substantial life insurance policies after retiring was to provide a pool of ready cash to deal with estate taxes so that other assets would not be drained. The 1981 tax reductions almost eliminate that need. As you have seen, the chances of your having any Federal estate tax depleting the capital you have accumulated has become remote.

In this book's first chapter, you saw the choices open to you in case you are still paying premiums on ordinary, cash value, life insurance. Now stop and do some serious thinking about *any type* of life insurance you still have. *What is its purpose?* Does it truly fill a need? How much additional current income could you enjoy if you stopped paying premiums and started investing that same amount of money? If you have a cash value life insurance policy and the continuing premiums are not a burden to you, you may decide that the cash it will produce for those you leave behind can be important to them. If that is the case, hold on, but do take a searching look at the cash values that have accumulated. Determine if they are capable of doing something more important for you if you borrow them and invest them for significant income or for growth opportunities — or if you might be better off having them applied to the purchase of a paid-up policy or extended term.

During your working years you may have had some low-cost group term insurance. In most instances you may have had the choice of simply dropping it or converting to cash value life insurance upon retirement. The conversion usually means very high premium costs since the premium is based on your age and life expectancy at retirement. Term policies, if they can be extended, are frequently discontinued at age seventy. If they go beyond that, the premium soars to awesome heights. One company presently charges $14,000 a year for a $100,000 term policy at age eighty. That is not exceptional. If you have group term through some source other than your former place of employment, by all means hold on to it for as long as they will permit, and for as long as the premiums are low.

Health and hospitalization. In the retirement years the gravest financial threat is the cost of illness. It is the gravest because your protection against the most serious, prolonged and costly circumstances caused by illness can fall disasterously short of being enough. The Department of Health and Human Services estimates that some 7 million families will spend more than 15 percent of their income on uninsured medical expense.

In the pre-retirement years, vast numbers of people have the mistaken notion that Social Security will provide all the retirement income needed and that Medicare will pay the costs of all illnesses and accidents after age 65. You have seen that Social Security doesn't come close to providing all the income needed, and the illusions about Medicare are equally wrong.

Medicare is a great help — up to a point. For people 65 years of age and older, *Medicare A* is free. It *helps* to pay the costs of hospitalization. It never was intended to pay all of the costs. As of 1981, if you are covered and are hospitalized, you pay the first $204 each year. You will have to pay more in succeeding years. Medicare then picks up the costs of the next 60 days. For the 30 days that follow, you are responsible for a good part of the costs and, thereafter, they all belong to you. You do have a *lifetime reserve* of an additional 60 covered days; once used, that reserve is gone. For any psychiatric care, while in the hospital, Medicare pays for the first $250 and you pay the balance. If you live at home and come to the hospital for out-patient therapy, 80 percent of the first $500 is covered by Medicare. There are additional specific limits, but those are the major ones. If you go to a skilled care nursing home, technically Medicare pays for the first 100 days. In actuality, the National Council of Health Centers states that the paid coverage is considerably less. Do not confuse *skilled nursing care homes* with *custodial nursing homes*. There is a vital difference. Medicare and most other health insurance policies cover some of the costs of a skilled nursing care facility, but they pay nothing at all towards the costs of a custodial nursing home. The distinction is that the skilled nursing care facility provides professional medical care. A nursing home is simply a place to live and there are no in-house doctors, registered nurses, etc. Fortunately, only about 5 percent of our population end up in nursing homes.

If you elect to pay for it, you can have *Medicare B*. The cost is about $130 a year, and the cost keeps rising. Medicare B pays for some doctor bills, some outpatient hospital care, some diagnostic tests, and some laboratory services. After you have paid the first $60 of physician and surgeon charges, each year, Medicare B pays 80 percent of *reasonable medical charges*. You pay the rest. The problem is that what Medicare defines as a *reasonable* charge may be quite a bit less than what your doctor considers reasonable for his or her services. It is entirely proper for you to question any doctor or surgeon, before treatment. Ask if they will accept Medicare *standard fees*.

Medigap insurance is your next defense. Medigap policies, made available by commercial insurance companies, pick up some of the differences between what Medicare pays and doesn't pay. There are various costs and benefits. The policies giving the broadest benefits charge about $350 a year. Typically, such a policy will pick up everything Medicare does not pay, for the first 60 days of hospitalization, and from 25 to 50 percent of the next 30 days. After that about 12 percent of hospital costs may be covered and 100 percent of in-hospital nursing care for stated periods of time.

Medicaid is at the end of the line. Medicaid is a joint Federal and state special assistance program. If you have exhausted all of your personal resources, Medicaid will take over. First you must have spent just about everything you have. You are allowed to maintain up to $100,000 of the value of your home. If one of a married couple is in need, one half of all income is deemed to belong to the other and may remain intact. There may be no efforts to transfer assets to children as a means of qualifying, nor may you sell off assets to family members at unrealistic prices. The requirements are tough, and they are rigid. The actual rules differ from state to state, and the trend has been to make them increasingly restrictive. Generally, those who are eligible for *SSI (Supplemental Security Income)* are also eligible for Medicaid.

Obviously, Medicaid is a desperation measure — truly the end of the line. The vital question is, *can you build any protection against the overwhelming expense that a catastrophic illness can incur?* Before retirement — yes, you can. You can buy major medical insurance capable of protecting you from medical costs of as much as one million dollars, even more. A number of companies make major medical available to employees as part of their group health and accident protection. Most executives have such policies. Some trade and professional and fraternal orders make it possible for members to have major medical policies.

Once you have retired, however, the story is different. Insurance companies are in business for profit. They have no interest in offering major medical protection to individuals aged 65 or more. The risks are too great.

The one answer appears to be: *keep yourself on the payroll.* This may mean that, company rules permitting, you must keep on working in the old job. If there is a compulsory retirement age perhaps you can remain under the group insurance plans by accepting a consultant's role. Check whatever associations you belong to, or may be able to join. Do any of them make major medical available to members? Are there any age restrictions?

Hospice care, a growing movement, can extend invaluable help in some of the most critical situations. The word *hospice* once had a single meaning — a place of refuge for travellers. Today the word hospice refers to a way of caring for people nearing the end of the journey through life, faced with dying and in need of refuge.

Hospice care is capable of dealing with a terminally ill person in ways that help to alleviate physical pain and, of equal or even greater importance, prepare the patient and those close to him or her, to face and accept the fact of death with mental and emotional understanding and control. Hospice care is also a means of greatly reducing the financial burdens involved.

There are hospice care divisions in some hospitals — there are independent hospice care facilities, but one of the strongest arms of the movement is the 24-hour a day availability of hospice care teams who come to the homes of those in need. The teams are composed of doctors, nurses, social workers, clergy, allied branches of the medical profession and lay volunteers.

The most important thing to appreciate about hospice care is that it is unlike traditional medical care. Doctors and their colleagues are dedicated to the curing of illness and the prolongation of life. Faced with a terminal type of cancer, for example, they will employ all of their skills, all of the technical equipment and all of the medication, surgery and other means of prolonging life at their command. In part these heroic measures are intended to extend the patient's life; in part they are for the perfection or creation of new techniques which may help others in the future. The extremes of treatment deal with the bodies of people, not with their emotions or with the emotions of the family. The measures employed entail enormous expense.

Hospice care is totally different. It accepts the fact that the illness is terminal and the entire effort is to ease pain and to permit the patient to accept the inevitable and to pass on with peace of mind and dignity. When a hospice team takes over, the effort generally is to keep the patient at home, not only for the far greater economies involved, but because the home environment makes far fewer emotional and physical demands on everyone involved. Where there is reason to move people to a hospice facility, there are significant economies compared with standard hospitalization. A hospice facility is considerably cheaper to build, equip, staff and maintain. Secondly, there is no need to use the vast array of equipment, sophisticated testing, diagnosis, treatment and life prolongation drugs.

To finance the hospice movement in this country, to bring it up to the broad level of acceptance and usage it has in England, there are several sources of funding being tapped: private donations, membership fees, hospital revenues, private and government grants, state and local contracts. Dr. Josefina Magno, who heads the National Hospice Organization, has said that most hospice care groups and facilities are non-profit and that, "No one should be denied hospice care for financial reasons."

There are between 300 and 500 hospice care facilities in the United States, and there is every indication that there will be more.

The Congressional Budget Office has said that more than one-third of the nation cannot afford a catastrophic illness or a chronic ailment that requires extensive medical care. The percentage, when applied to people in retirement, is much higher.

Some people, in their efforts to build defenses against this frightening threat, buy cancer insurance protection. The Health Insurance Association of America points out that cancer insurance protects against that single disease and the statistics show that only 1 person in 220 ever becomes a cancer patient. Those are long odds. In addition, many cancer policies will not pay any of the costs of ailments that are side effects of cancer.

There are some indications that the government and some insurance companies are looking for ways to shield people, particularly those in retirement, from being destroyed financially by a major illness. The existing lack of adequate protection underscores the immense importance of pre-retirement planning that strives to build assets capable of dealing with this grave problem.

Chapter Eleven

"But, I have no capital!"

"**B**ut," you say, "I have no way of increasing my income — no way of building a base for new income — *I have no capital.*" Maybe you have unrecognized — hidden capital. Many people do.

Throughout this book a variety of ways of uncovering concealed capital and putting it to work have been discussed.

Hidden savings

1. *If you have cash value life insurance:* You have a number of choices. If you see a genuine need to maintain a life insurance policy you can ask that your cash values be used:

A.   —to buy paid-up life. You'll have a somewhat smaller policy but you pay no more premiums. The money you had been sending to the insurance company becomes extra income for you —capital you can put to work.

B. Your cash values can buy extended term. The face value remains the same. You may outlive the policy, or you may not, depending on the amount of cash value and your own future health and good fortune. Again, no more money to the insurance company. You have new income — new capital.

If you conclude that you really don't need to keep your life insurance policy, cancel it. Take the cash value. You will have a block of capital you can put to work.

If you are prepared to continue with the policy and the premium payments, borrow the cash value. It can be earning money for you. See page 23 for detail.

2. *If you have life insurance of any kind* for the purpose of handling eventual estate taxes, take a long look at what the 1981 tax revisions have accomplished in that area. By the time we reach 1987 the estate of a married person will have to be more than a million dollars before there is *any* estate tax. For a single individual, the amount will have to be $600,000 or more. If you no longer have a need for that type of protection, cancel. You'll have those premium dollars as extra money to spend. See pages 24 and 212 for detail.

3. *Disability insurance.* Disability insurance is an immensely important form of protection during the years of earning. It replaces the income that is lost if a serious disability creates a temporary or permanent loss of earned income. Once you have retired, however, there is no lost income if you become disabled. Cancel.

4. *If you are now reinvesting in anything* — savings or any stocks or mutual funds — and you need more spending money, STOP. You are sending money ahead for future use and unless inflation quits, you are guaranteeing that the money you could be using today will buy considerably less in the days ahead. See page 22 for detail.

5. *If you are not age 72 yet* and have accepted a contract as a regularly paid consultant, and are not called on to work on a regular basis, you may be needlessly surrendering tax-free Social Security benefits. See page 46 for detail.

6. *If you have a substantial equity in your home* but are short of dollars for your daily needs:

    A. You can stay in your home and, when conditions are right, arrange to obtain a *reverse mortgage* which will provide you with a new source of monthly income. See page 148 for detail.

    B. *A sale/leaseback* is a method of selling your house, retaining the right to live in it and creating a new source of income. See page 149 for detail.

    C. *A life estate agreement* arranged in cooperation with a recognized charity, university, hospital, etc., can either end existing mortgage payments, or give you a block of capital to invest. At the same time it will establish a charitable tax deduction that will reduce your taxes for as long as six years. And the greatest benefit is that you'll be able to stay in your home for as long as you or your spouse may live. See page 156 for detail.

    D. A *charitable remainder trust* gives you the opportunity to donate any asset...your home, other real estate, securities, etc., to a recognized non-profit organization in a way that will provide generous income on the total current value, undiluted by any taxes, for as long as you, or you and your spouse may live. It also enables you to take substantial tax deductions for as long as six years. You have the choice of taking your income as an unchanging sum each month, or a flexible amount that is capable of reacting to continuing inflation by giving you the equivalent of cost of living increases. See page 159 for detail.

E. You sell your home and you plan to buy a new one, but you find that the down payment and monthly mortgage payments will leave you without the extra spending money you hoped the sale of your home would make possible. Your answer may be to make a mutually beneficial arrangement with one or more of your children. You and your spouse can take advantage of the annual exclusion that permits a couple to give away as much as $20,000 a year to each of as many people as they wish, free of gift tax. Make a sufficient gift to your children. They will use it as the down payment on the new home and will assume the mortgage payments. You pay them just enough rent to cover their after tax monthly costs. The net result is your monthly outlay is far less than it would be otherwise, giving you income for other purposes. Your children will be buying a home at a bargain price and can anticipate that, in time, they'll have a sizeable profit. See page 162 for detail.

7. *There are a multitude of ways to earn money* during retirement years.

A. Barter can be your means of attaining many things without spending money. Reviewing your skills, your favorite activities and those things you would enjoy doing, in terms of filling the needs of others, provides a fresh viewpoint. You will see myriad opportunities to exchange something you can provide for something someone else can provide. You may discover that there is a Barter Exchange in your community that will help you and others to match up what you want and what you can give. See page 61 for detail.

B. Are you a craftsman? There are opportunities for people with manual skills to derive income as well as pleasure from what they can produce. See page 59 for detail.

8. *Are you fearful of invading capital?* You may be seriously shortchanging yourself. Inflation at the level we have known throughout recent years has forced a massive change in attitudes about using some of your capital as opposed to relying solely on income. It is a subject to be studied with great care. You may find that a well planned invasion of capital can make a remarkable difference in your financial ability to live as you want to live. See page 17 for detail.

9. *Are you clinging to investments* that do too little or nothing for you? Sentiment, uncertainty, fear, unjustified optimism and just plain lack of understanding are factors that lead many to the costly error of holding on to investments that should be eliminated. Capital gains tax liability has often been viewed as a reason for not selling an investment that has grown in value but pays no dividends, or pays small dividends. Today capital gains taxes are so favorable that they should not bar the sale. The most expensive mistake you can make is to let yourself be frozen to any investment that fails to give you the yields you could get were you to sell and move the after-tax dollars to greener fields. See page 17 for detail.

Epilogue

There is a Battle to be Fought

Holding your head above the economic tides in time of ever increasing living costs, towering interest rates and punitive taxation is not easy for anyone. Retirement brings with it added problems.

To be fearful of what may lie ahead if inflation continues to be our constant companion, and to be seriously disturbed when a dependable source of income proves to be less than dependable are natural. In moderation, fear and worry are healthy. They inspire thought and investigation. And they motivate.

It is our great good fortune that we enjoy a free enterprise system because we have economic freedom. In almost every conceivable way we are free to control our economic lives. We are:

- *free* to choose ways of earning money on a full or part-time basis — as an employee, an employer, or independently
- *free* to choose our means of accumulating capital

229

- *free* to select our own sources of interest, dividends and profits
- *free* to regulate the degree of risk we will accept
- *free* to build defenses against known and unknown threats to what assets we have and to our financial future
- *free* to conserve what we have
- *free* to take advantage of legal ways to avoid, reduce, or defer taxes
- *free* to control and dispose of our assets so that they will flow where and how we wish.

This is an impressive list of personal financial freedoms. What you have read in this book provides you with another long list of measures that take full advantage of all of these freedoms.

You have a significant advantage. The fact that you have read *The Retirement Money Book* is evidence that you realize you're engaged in a serious battle against inflation...that the future does *not* take care of itself. Your financial future is in your hands. How you will live the rest of your life, to a great extent, is dependent on you, your decisions, and your actions now.

To read about the things you can do...to think about them...to discuss them are essential steps. They are meaningless, however, *unless you act*. Decide which steps to take first. Decide where to turn for help in putting those ideas to work. If you need a financial planner, an investment advisor, a securities broker, a real estate agent, an insurance agent, or a banker, or all of them, get them now. If you don't know particular specialists, pick up your phone. Call friends or business people you trust and get their recommendations. Find out which professionals have demonstrated sound knowledge, dedication and integrity. Then go to those professionals. Tell them what you have decided to do. Give them your confidence. And hold nothing back. The more information you provide, the greater their ability to serve you. Tell them you want action *now*.

Time is a vital factor. It is your ally if you use it, but your enemy if you waste it. Every day your capital is earning maximum return is a plus. Every day it is working for starvation wages is a loss. You must cut the losses and build the plusses.

Yes, you have a serious battle on your hands. But you are armed with knowledge. You are armed with many actions you can take. The battle can be won. It *will* be won *if you act now*.

Glossary

Although every effort has been made to avoid technical language, there are certain words and terms that do appear in the text that may be unfamiliar. As an aid to fuller understanding there follows an alphabetical listing of those "possibilities". The explanations that follow each word or term apply to the way they are used in the book. For example: while *bullion* is a soup, it is not the kind of bullion we are talking about in the text; *appreciation* we all know as a synonym for gratitude but while the kind of appreciation we have dealt with may inspire gratitude in our usage, it refers to profit.

All Saver Certificate — The tax laws passed in the latter part of 1981 included the granting to banks and savings and loan institutions of the right to issue this special certificate giving the investor up to $1,000 of tax-free income ($2,000 per married couple) on interest equal to 70 percent of the average investment yield of Treasury bills. The certificates have a one year maturity and will be available until December 31, 1982. Rates will be determined each month and will be firm for one full year.

Annual Exclusion — The Internal Revenue permits you to give away up to $10,000 each year ($20,000 per couple) to as many people as you choose without creating any gift tax liability.

Annualized Yield — Based on the current dividend or interest, the percentage of annual yield you can anticipate if the rate remains the same.

Annuities — Contracts sold by insurance companies involving certain forms of guaranteed income in return for money paid to them. The amount of income is based on the amount in the account at the time payouts start, the annuitant's age and the payout option selected. A particular attraction is that earnings in the account are tax-deferred until payouts start.

Deferred annuities are those that are purchased with a lump sum or on an accumulation basis but postpone payouts until some time in the future.

Fixed annuities are those that pay an unchanging number of dollars.

Immediate annuities provide that payouts start at the time of purchase.

Variable annuities provide monthly payouts that are capable of increasing or decreasing, reflecting the performance of an investment portfolio.

Wrap-around annuities generally are available when an insurance company and a mutual fund group combine forces, and the annuitant is permitted to elect which type of mutual fund is to be used as the investment base, with the right to move from one type of fund to others at will.

Annuitizing — The start of payouts being sent to a

deferred annuity investor constitutes the *annuitizing* of the contract.

Appreciation Potential — Opportunity for profit.

Bargain Sale — The sale of an asset to a recognized charitable organization at a price below the true market value is recognized by IRS and is a means of making a tax deductible charitable donation.

Blind Pool — A real estate limited partnership syndication may sell participations on the basis of making investments in various real estate ventures. Until all of the money is in hand no specific investments are made.

Bond Maturities — Bonds have specific life spans. At the end of the time period the issuer redeems the bond, paying the full face value and any accrued interest.

Break Points — Where sales charges are involved, as in the purchase of some mutual funds, the charges are reduced as the amount invested increases. The dollar amounts at which these reductions occur are referred to as the *break points*.

Capital Invasion — Using a part of one's capital in addition to whatever interest or dividends the capital produces.

Cash Flow — The total of the dividends, interest payments, realized profits and any return of principal received by you constitutes your cash flow.

Cash Values — The accumulation of that part of premium payments on certain types of life insurance policies that constitute the "savings portions".

Closely Held Company — A corporation whose stock is owned primarily or entirely by a few people, by one family, or by one individual.

Collectibles — Art, fine jewelry, rare coins, rare books, oriental rugs, antiques and similar assets which one may invest in, hoping for profits.

Commodity Futures — The purchase of contracts to buy or sell precious metals or agricultural products at specific future times at specific prices.

Convertible Securities — An income producing security that gives its owner the right to trade-in that security for another type of security issued by the same company if and when the other security reaches a pre-determined price.

Covered Option — An investor selling an option to buy a certain stock by a specified date is a covered option if the seller owns the stock at the time the option is sold.

Debt Securities — Securities that are, in fact, loans with guarantees of certain interest payment and repayment of the securities' value by a fixed date, as opposed to securities such as common stocks which give the investor a share in any part of earnings paid out as dividends.

Discretionary Accounts — This type of account exists when an investor turns money or other assets over to an investment advisor or broker giving him the full right to buy and sell securities without further consultation or authorization.

Equity — The ownership interest which common and preferred stockholders have in a company.

Exchange Privilege — When a mutual fund is one of a group of funds under the management of a single company, the shareholder in any one of the funds has the right to exchange those shares for shares of equal value of any of the other funds in the group. Generally this is done for a minimal fee of about $5 or without charge.

Fixed Annuity — An annuity contract that provides

that the payout will consist of an unchanging number of dollars at regular intervals.

Funding — When a trust or an annuity account is established, for example, it is essential that money be invested in something that will provide income. The investment is the means of *funding* the arrangement.

Gold Bullion — A brick, wafer or ingot of gold.

Growth Stocks — Those common stocks that have characteristics that make them logical candidates for possible increases in value. The factors may be the company's history of investing substantial portions of their earnings in research and development and a record of steadily and rapidly increasing earnings over a period of time.

Illiquidity — The lack of ease in selling any type of investment.

Immediate Annuity — An annuity contract that starts making monthly payments to the annuitant immediately.

Income Averaging — A right granted by the Internal Revenue Code, in some situations, that permits a person to pay taxes on a sum of cash received in one year as though it had been received over a number of years — 5 or 10 years in specific cases — materially reducing the tax liability.

Invasion of Capital — Taking portions of one's underlying investment over and above any interest or dividend income the investment produces.

Krugerrands — A south African coin containing exactly one ounce of gold.

Leverage — Using borrowed money in the effort to realize greater return from an investment. Both the chances for gain or loss are increased.

Life Estate Agreement — A legal arrangement with a recognized charity or other non-profit organization whereby a home may be donated with the understanding that the donor, or donor and other persons, have the right to live in the home for the remainder of his/her or their lives.

Listed Securities — Securities that are registered with and bought and sold on a recognized exchange such as the New York Stock Exchange.

Locked-In Yield — A bond, for example, is purchased with the knowledge that it will pay a specific, unchanging amount of interest for a period of years. The yield, thus, is securely *locked-in.*

Money-At-Risk — In real estate limited partnerships the limited partners have the advantage of being permitted to base tax deductions on a combination of the dollars they have invested plus money borrowed by the general partners. Loans in such cases are called *"non-recourse" loans*, meaning that the limited partners have no liability for the money borrowed even if it is not repaid. In all other types of tax-sheltered investments, Internal Revenue does not permit deductions to be taken on anything but the money actually invested — the *money-at risk.*

Non-Recourse Loans — See above.

Numismatic Value — Beyond the value of any precious metal in a coin, there is a further value based on the scarcity and the condition of the coin. These additional factors comprise the *numismatic value.*

Options — An individual may buy or sell the right to buy a specific stock at a specific price by a specific date.

Over-The-Counter-Market — Those securities that are not bought and sold on the various stock exchanges are bought and sold in the *over-the-counter-market.* This consists of investment dealers scattered across the nation who will deal in these "unlisted" securities over the telephone. Many strong and large companies choose not to have their securities listed and these, along with the securities of smaller companies, are available through the over-the-counter market. It is the principal market for federal and municipal bonds.

Portfolio of Securities — When an individual, a corporation or any other type of organization owns a variety of securities, the total package of securities is referred to as the "portfolio".

Preferred Stock — A company is obligated to pay dividends to its *preferred stock* shareholders before payments are made to holders of common stock. If the company fails, the preferred stockholders are first in line to collect any remaining assets.

Price-Earnings Ratio — Divide a stock's annual earnings into the price of one share and you have the *price-earnings ratio*. For example: if the price of ACF Corp is $20 per share and the company's earnings for the year amounted to $2 a share the price-earnings ratio would be 10 to 1.

Remainder Interest — This is a term used by IRS; it relates to the way in which one arrives at the tax deduction one may take when donating property to a charity by means of a trust providing that certain beneficiaries are to receive life-long income from the value of the property donated. *Remainder interest* is arrived at through the application of a formula that takes into consideration the dollar value of income to be received by the beneficiaries, based on their sex and ages. This is subtracted from the current market value of the gift, and the balance constitutes the deduction allowable.

Reverse Mortgage — As an example, a thrift institution approached by someone with a fully paid home will lend up to 80 percent of the home's value; will buy an annuity with that money; have the interest due the lender deducted and the balance paid the home owner each month.

Roll-Over (Retirement Plan) — When a tax-sheltered retirement plan terminates, the money paid to the individual would be taxable in the year received unless the recipient elects to take advantage of the right to put that sum into an Individual Retirement Account. Rolling-over the plan proceeds in that manner retains the tax deferral on both the money involved and whatever it may earn.

Roll-Over (Home sale and purchases) — Those who sell their homes at a profit and who, within two years, buy and occupy a new home costing as much or more than they received have no capital gains tax liability. This *roll-over* privilege may be employed as often as one wishes. For those who are aged 55 or over the right to realize up to $125,000 of profit tax-free when selling their homes is a once-in-a-lifetime right.

Sale/Leaseback — An arrangement wherein one's home is sold at a steep discount below current prices, but the seller is permitted to live on in the house, paying a mutually agreeable monthly rental. Meanwhile, the buyer, in addition to making a down payment, purchases an annuity on the seller's life, providing life-long monthly income.

Secondary Market — As an illustration, a tax-free municipal bond unit investment trust is available for purchase by the public. There are a fixed number of units for sale, and when they have been bought no more are made available. From then on those who bought the units may, if they choose, sell their units or buy units from other investors through investment firms. This second area of buying and selling is the *secondary market.*

Stock Dividend — There are times when some companies will choose to pay regular or extra dividends to their shareholders by issuing shares of the company's stock.

Stock Splits — For any of a number of reasons, the directors of a corporation may decide to reduce the market price of their shares by splitting the stock, issuing two shares for each share outstanding (or three-for-one, etc.) When a two-for-one split takes place, for instance, shares that were worth $40 each assume a new value of $20 each, but each shareholder owns twice as many shares.

Street Name — Brokerage firms and the trust departments of banks, with the consent of their clients, often will register a person's securities in the company's name instead of in the name of the true owner. This is done to facilitate trading, particularly where an investor has a margin account or when the investor prefers that his/her securities be held in safekeeping by the broker or bank.

Tax Avoidance — Tax *evasion* is criminal. *Tax avoidance* refers to fully legal steps that may be taken to eliminate tax liabilities. Investing in tax-free municipal bonds, as an example, *avoids* any tax liability.

Tax Brackets — Federal and state taxes are on a sliding scale based on one's taxable income. The more income, the greater the percentage of it is taxed. Thus, the determination of what your annual taxable income amounts to pin-points the percentage that must be paid. That percentage is your tax bracket.

Tax Deferral — Tax laws recognize a variety of forms of investment that permit the investor to postpone the payment of taxes on the money invested, or on the earnings of those investments, until some time in the future. The tax liability is *deferred*.

Tax Shelters — Any investment that gives the investor the legal right to avoid, reduce or defer tax liabilities constitutes a *tax shelter*.

Total Return — When an investment provides dividends and the possibilities of profits, lumping the two together constitutes *total return* on the investment.

Unit Trusts — A trust is created for the purpose of investing in a portfolio of securities. It then divides the total portfolio into multiple units so that they can be offered to the public at relatively moderate cost.

Variable Annuity — An annuity contract that provides that the annuitant's income is to be based on a fixed percentage of an investment portfolio's varying value, thus giving the annuitant monthly income that will increase or decrease. This is in contrast with a fixed annuity which provides an unchanging number of dollars each month.

Withdrawal Plan — A service offered by mutual funds which provides that after the investor has a certain minimum amount in the account ($5,000 in many cases), he or she may instruct the fund to pay out regular sums of money at specified intervals — monthly, quarterly, etc. The amount of money requested does not reflect the fund's true yield or its total return but is an arbitrary sum. The payments are made by the fund by liquidating whatever number of full and fractional share are required to fulfill the amount requested. Unlike an annuity, if all of the shares are used in this process, the account and the payments come to an end. Also, unlike an annuity, any assets remaining in the account, should the annuitant die, is the property of the annuitant's estate. The funds generally make no charge for the service, and the investor's specifications may be changed whenever he or she wishes.

Wrap-Around Annuity — This is a financial product made possible by the combining of an insurance company's annuity contract and a mutual fund organization providing the funding via the various funds under its management. The annuitant has the right to specify which of the mutual funds are to be employed for his/her account and has the further privilege of being free to order changes from one fund to another as often as he/she wishes prior to annuitizing and once a year after that time. (At publication this concept is under attack by IRS and some changes in its structure are anticipated.)

Yield — The return realized from an investment.

Index